AF241790

AS WE THINKETH SO ARE WE

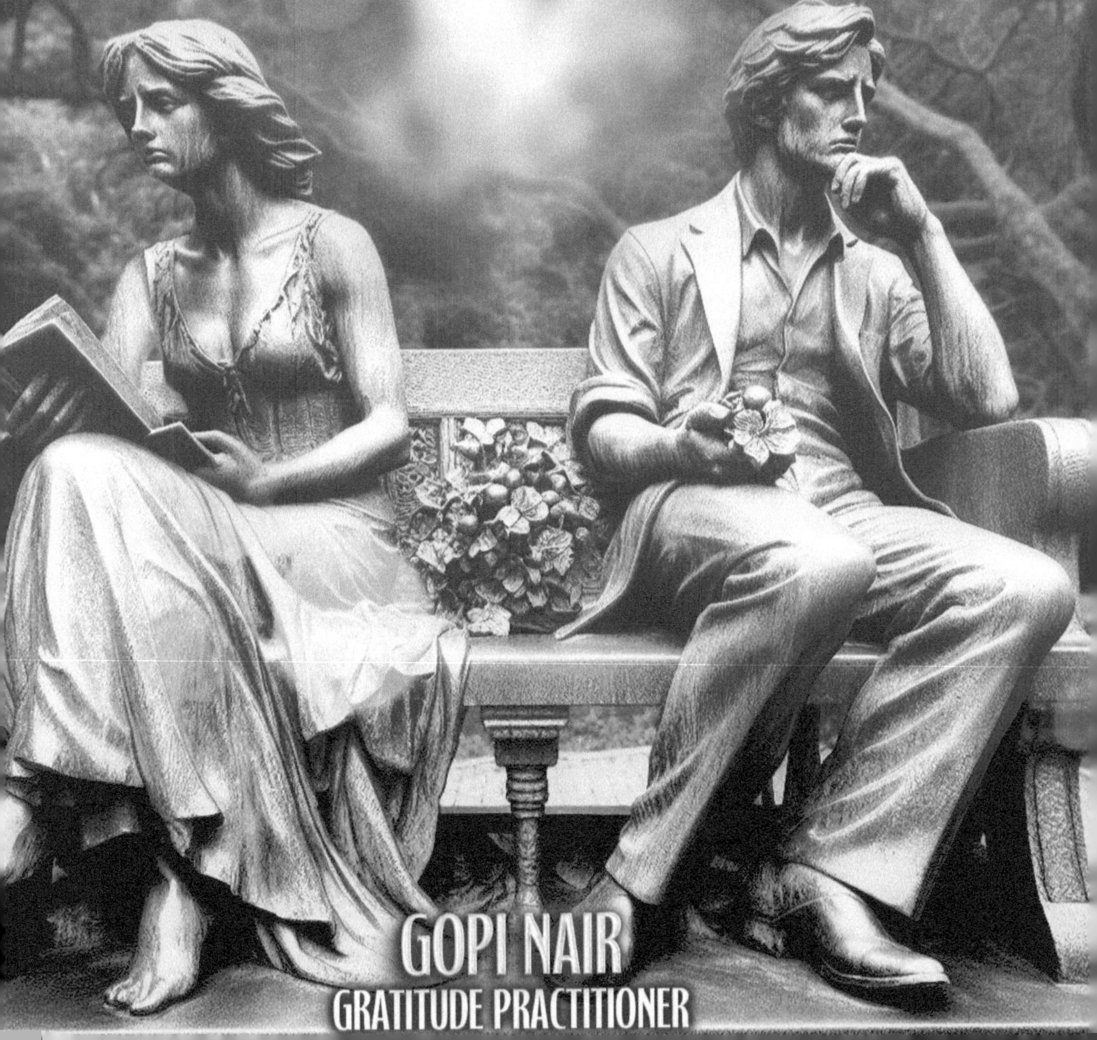

GOPI NAIR

Hotline: 630-290-6847

Email: gopi132@yahoo.com

Address: 776 Stratford Ave, Elmhurst, IL 60126, USA

Ordering Information:

Quantity sales. Special discounts are available on quantity purchases by corporations, associations, and others. For details, contact the publisher at the address above.

ISBN: 978-1-962484-35-0 (Paperback Version)
978-1-962484-37-4 (Digital Version)

Rev. Date: 09/03/2024

As We Thinketh

So Are We
As Above, So Below
As Within, So Without

Gopi Nair
Gratitude Practitioner

Table of Contents

My Hearty Gratitude

I take this opportunity to express my gratitude to the luminaries and great thinkers who left their spiritual footprints in the timeless Universe.

Gopi.

A Note to my Readers

I am deeply indebted to every reader who invested their valuable time to read this book.

Many stories and concepts are repeated more than once throughout this book. This was done with the purpose of cementing the ideas in the mind of the reader.

I urge the readers to read this book at least three times and apply at least one idea in your everyday life to improve the quality of life.

After all, repetition is the mother of perfection.

Best Regards,

Gopi.

This book is lovingly dedicated to Niam, Asher and Kriya, my three grandchildren who remind me of my own awareness.

ACKNOWLEDGEMENT

This is to express my deepest gratitude to the people behind, who helped me finish my book.

Ms. Andy Anderson, my Sales Consultant and to my Production team - Ms. Cherry McNeill and Cliff Kerbie Gurrea.

I will be forever grateful.

-Gopi-

CHAPTER I

Thought Power

We all think during our waking hours. Our thoughts guide our speech, and our speech results in action. The sum total of our actions creates our world. If our thoughts are positive, they create positive speech and positive actions. Conversely, negative thoughts produce negative speech, which leads to negative actions.

This book will help you manage your thoughts on a daily basis to improve the quality of your life. Having understood the power of thought, you will cease to blame others for your plight. Instead, you will begin to take command of your ship of destiny and navigate it successfully through the sea of life. You will no longer be a victim of circumstances; instead, like a master weaver, you will begin to weave your own circumstances. You will not be blaming destiny but will engage in changing it, thought by thought, speech by speech, and deed by deed.

Basic Building Block

Just like an atom is the basic building block of matter, thought is the basic building block of spirit—the primordial energy out of which the universe has emerged. The science of creation and the art of creativity, we must master in order to recreate our universe. You do not have to recreate your universe, if you are actually contented with your present state of affairs called life. But if you do not like what you have, you have been endowed with the power to change it. You are indeed the architect of destiny, the author of the book of life, and the great transformer who is capable of bringing total change into your life. History is filled with stories of great movers and shakers who not only transformed their individual lives, but also totally changed the world they lived in. People like Mahatma Gandhi, Mother Theresa, Abraham Lincoln, and Martin Luther King are some of the examples of great transformers who did not like what they saw. They changed the world by simply becoming the very change they envisioned. We, too, have the same opportunity; we, too, enjoy the same power of thinking; and we, too, have all the tools of transformation at our beck and call. The only thing lacking in us is the awareness that we, indeed, are the architects of our own destiny.

Awareness

Awareness is the mother of conscious behavior. Every thought we think, every word we utter, and every deed we do should be the outcome of conscious behavior and not an accidental outburst. A discipline in our thinking, a discipline in our speaking, and a discipline in our action alone can generate constant awareness. A man of constant awareness is always in control of his thoughts, his speech, and his deeds. In such a person, we will witness heavenly harmony and an inexplicable tranquility.

Cultivating constant awareness is as easy as counting one, two, and three. Awareness belongs to thought awareness, speech awareness, and action awareness—the three stages of evolution in human behavior. Consciously, one can cultivate awareness in all three stages of behavior. It requires practice, dedication, and more practice.

Thought Awareness

There are multiple thoughts vying for each other to get our attention, and left unattended, they create a stampede, resulting in intolerable stress. Human beings fall sick as their physical bodies fail to cope with the tension created by their intruding thoughts. In medical language, the doctors call it a "nervous breakdown." But with regular training, one can manage these thoughts, and they all will behave to create a harmonious mind. A harmonious mind alone can generate ceaseless peace and tranquility in one's life. Thought management is like any other task, and it becomes easier with practice.

Basically, there are two sources of thoughts coming into one's mind:

1. External
2. Internal

All our sense organs are "messengers," carrying messages to the brain. While you are driving on the road, you see a big fire, which can stimulate thoughts in your mind. It can trigger a memory of a fire one witnessed in childhood. Or it can bring a voice from the past: "Son, stay away from fire," your mother told you when you were a child. This is an example of an external source of thought.

The internal source of thought comes from the subconscious repository or memory bank. All our thoughts are stored in the subconscious mind, and from that storehouse emerge thoughts, many times without notice. You are preparing for an important test, a licensing exam, and all of a sudden you thought about the first test you took in the first grade, where you got a 100%. All of a sudden, you were flown into the past, and you felt the excitement of your teacher and the parents congratulating you. You travelled into history, and "relived" every moment of that experience.

Speech Awareness

The second element of human behavior is speech. Most of us talk like "talking machines," and many times, we get in trouble for the uncontrolled use of words and then say sorry. If you are aware of the words you speak, many of our day-to-day problems can be avoided. Many people have a "silver tongue," and of course, they were not born with that.

"Life and death are in the power of the tongue," proclaims the Bible. If you are aware of the words you speak, it will help you manage your thoughts better. As a matter of fact, thought management begins with speech management. Remind yourself to be aware of every word that comes out of you. After a while, it becomes second nature to you without effort; you seem to possess a "silver tongue."

Action Awareness

The culmination of every thought and speech results in a corresponding action. Many times, we may not be able to trace it to a particular thought or speech, but definitely, we all act as a result of our thought and the corresponding speech. Thus, thought awareness and speech awareness give us a handle over our actions. A disciplined person always has very disciplined behavior.

TSA Alignment

Thought, Speech, and Action Alignment (TSA) is the secret of harmony. It is very hard to come by, yet with regular practice, one can create a state of mind where thought, speech, and action align themselves like a harmonious planetary alignment. As a man thinketh, he speaketh, he acteth, and he becometh. Hence, the Biblical expression, "As a man thinketh, so is he."

As Above, So Below; As Within, So Without

The ancient emerald tablet, which was found to be more than five thousand years old, proclaimed this truth: "As Above, So Below, As Within, So Without." It means as your thoughts (offspring of spirit), so are your circumstances. We are all told that man is the creature of circumstances. To a great extent, it is correct, but once you understand the principle of creation, by molding your thoughts, you can create your own destiny. If plants and trees are allowed to grow wild, they create an unruly forest, whereas if they are planted with a plan, and attended to regularly by trimming and removing the dead ones, one can create a beautiful garden. The difference between a wild forest and a beautiful garden is proper planning and attentiveness. You are a creature of circumstances without thought management, and you change your own circumstances (thus becoming a creator of circumstances) if you manage your thoughts with understanding. Most of us go through life like "sleepwalkers," not knowing what we are thinking, speaking, and doing. Our family, our "society," our school, and the country we live in have programmed us in certain ways. Breaking out of that orthodoxy of pseudo-puritanism requires spiritual stamina which almost all of us lack. The sole purpose of this book is to give you the spiritual stamina you need to break out of the prison of intellectual slavery.

Know Your Universe

Our universe is a gigantic network of energy. We are all connected by this energy network. Any student of physics will know the three principles of energy. They are:

1. Energy cannot be created.
2. Energy cannot be de destroyed.
3. Energy can only be transformed.

> "In the beginning, there was the word (spoken energy), the word was with God (primordial energy), and the word was God (pure energy)." —New Testament

The same thought was echoed in the Rig Veda, the oldest written scripture known to mankind. It says:

> *Om! Poornamidam, Poornamadam*
> *Poornad, Poornamudachyate*
> *Poornasya, Poornamadaya*
> *Poornameva, Avasishyate!*
> (Sanskrit)

Translated into English, it means:

"This is infinite. That is infinite. From infinite comes infinite. If you take away infinite from infinite, infinite alone remains." Just like the drop of water from the Pacific Ocean has all the properties of ocean water, life forms, wherever you see them, have the same attributes of an immeasurable life force. A lighted match stick, though very tiny, contains the fiery attributes of a thunderbolt, and it is enough to cause a wildfire to burn down a whole country. Understand the truth that life force is filled with potency, and the size we see is inconsequential. A giant oak tree waits in the acorn to be summoned to come out of the seed and fulfill its purpose. There is a seed of life force in each form of life, including human beings. While all other life forms are governed by their instincts, man alone is endowed with the power of discrimination, which is seated in memory. Using the power of discrimination, we can transform our lives in any way we choose. We are already doing it, though most of us seldom realize it.

There are three things we must know about our universe. They are:

1. The universe is impersonal and eternal.
2. The universe reciprocates in kind—many fold.
3. You are the universe!

You can compare the universe with the Pacific Ocean. It is very impersonal. Many people living in San Francisco go surfing, play with the waves, and enjoy riding in excitement. But if somebody does not know surfing and gets carried away by the strong waves, you cannot blame the ocean. It is as impersonal as a tree, a rock, or the Himalayas. It is also eternal, as it does not exist in the field of time.

Our universe is like electricity, which favors those who know the principles of electricity. Those who do not know the principles of current flow could get electricuted. Nobody says that electricity is to blame for such accidents. Similarly, if we understand the principles that govern the universe, we can very well draw its favor, or if not, we will be punished by the impersonal universe. Using our own intelligence, we obey the principles, and the very principles obey us, and we accomplish the unthinkable and the unattainable feats in the world.

Another important attribute of the universe is that it reciprocates in kind—many fold. Whatever we give to the universe, it will give it back multiplied. A farmer sows one seed of wheat; he gets a harvest—not one seed back. This is a very important principle of the universe to bear in mind. The theory of the law of karma is based on this principle of the universe. Simply put, this means "what goes around comes around"—many fold. On a positive note, if you do an act of kindness to anyone or anything in the universe, it will come back to you in kind several times. The only difference is that it may not come back to you from the same person or the same place, it can come back from any part of the body of the universe which is infinite. So be careful what you think, what you say, or what you do. Every thought, speech, and action has its own consequence, and it is, indeed, a boomerang.

The third principle summarizes the first two to reveal a secret. Indeed, you are the universe! Nothing happens outside of you. Whatever you think forms your speech, and whatever you speak becomes a command to produce the corresponding action. Thus, your thought, speech, and action create, brick by brick—rather, thought by thought—the universe that you are. In other words, the universe that you have is the effect of your thoughts.

Law of Cause and Effect

The law of cause and effect states that:

1. Every effect has a cause.
2. If you remove the cause, the effect disappears.
3. Do not work on the effect to change the cause.

Following the law of cause and effect, we should not work on the effects. We should work on the primary cause that produced the undesirable effect. If we do not like our universe, we must go within and change our thoughts—the primary cause that created our universe. Most of us always fight the circumstances and seldom succeed, as the cause remains unattended and unchanged. If you want to change the world outside, you have to change the world inside—the birthing chamber of the cause.

Circumstances simply reveal our true nature to ourselves. It is a "looking glass" through which you can get a clear picture of your own real personality. We all become that which we secretly harbor in our minds. For example, a man wants to be wealthy, and all his life, from dawn to dusk, he is thinking ill of people with wealth. He ridicules them, saying that all the wealth they have accumulated came from dubious means. He simply cannot stand wealthy people. How do you expect such a man to be wealthy? It is like a man who wants to reach the east, and walks towards the west, and complains that he did not reach the east. Anything you criticize will stay away from you, and that which you praise will love to be with you. So if you want to be wealthy, think of wealth and release it with joy; it will come back to you multiplied. When you focus your thought, speech, and actions on your very desire, you will gravitate towards its fulfillment.

CHAPTER II

The Science and Art of Creation

In the first chapter, we got a glimpse of the universe and the principles that govern our lives in the universe. After knowing that the very nature of the universe is energy, and that we are, ourselves, the universe, it is easy to conclude that the principles governing energy are the same principles that govern our own being. There was a dialogue between a Hindu master and his disciple when the master said, "Son, there is only one difference between you and me. You think you are in this world, but I think the world is in me." Indeed, you are the world! You are not in this world.

The Science of Creation says that there is unappropriated energy that can be transformed into any form (appropriated energy) by the use of willpower. In the law of electricity, there is a principle of transformation called the power of orientation. No matter how much electricity you have, it will not move without the intervention of the power of orientation. As soon as the power of orientation is introduced, it will induce the energy flow. Similarly, the unappropriated energy we see around us will not be transformed without the intervention of the agency of human willpower. In Sanskrit, it is called the *"ichasakti"*—power of desire. The simple chart below will explain the science of creation:

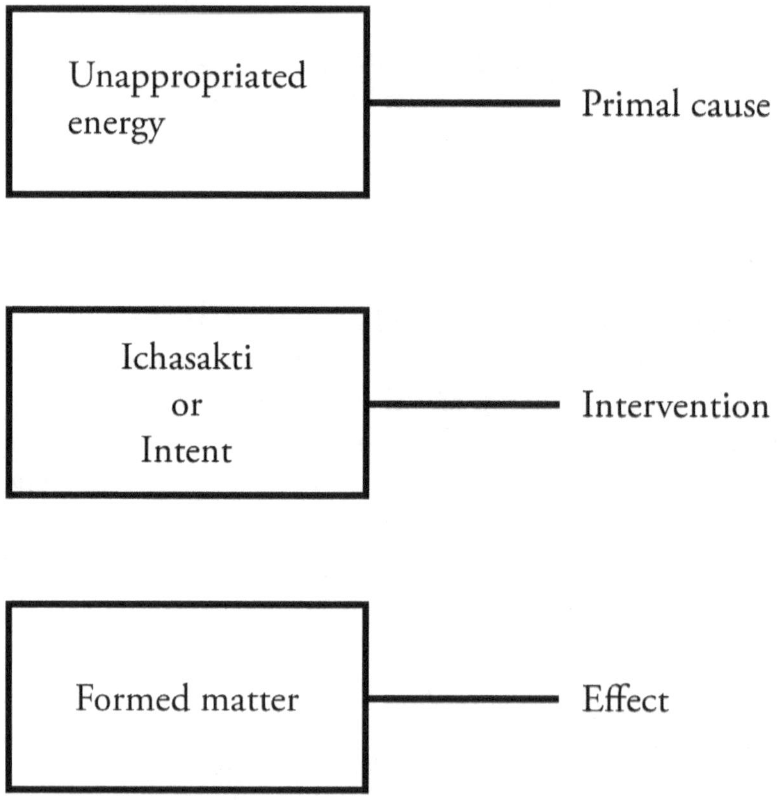

called the *"ichasakti"*—power of desire. The simple chart below will explain the science of creation:

A Burning Desire

A burning desire is the beginning of creation. Once you know what you want, half the battle is won. Most of us go through life without knowing what we want. Like a wooden plank caught in the high seas, we waste our energy and life going thither and hither, floating aimlessly in the sea of life. With the curiosity of a child, the zeal of a missionary, and the dedication of a mother, we must have the ability to translate our burning desire into reality. The world is grateful to countless men and women who preceded us, who dreamed lofty dreams, and who gave their lives towards the achievement of their goal. A Columbus, a Michelangelo, a Mahatma Gandhi, a Mother Theresa, or an Abraham Lincoln, a Gautama Buddha, or a Jesus Christ would not have become what they were but for their ideal of a better world. They were consumed with a passion for their cause; they gave everything they had to change this world. Lord Buddha was right when he said that you become what you think all day long.

Your Dominant Thoughts

Your dominant thoughts dictate the goal of your life, whether you like it or not. If you do not like the world you have, look at your dominant thoughts. Are they wrapped in negativity? What thoughts do you harbor in secrecy? What are your fears? Are they becoming your reality? Do you hold hatred for anybody? Answers to many of these questions define where the fault lines lie in your life.

The personality you have today is the sum total of the dominant thoughts you entertain in the secret corridors of your mind, and nobody except you has a clear picture of them. A self-examination of those thoughts, and most importantly, a determination to remove those self-defeating thoughts from your mental plane are crucial to reshaping your destiny. Now that you know the science behind the art of creation, you can change the course of your life.

Quality of Thought

The quality of your thoughts defines the quality of your life. You can change a life of gripping fear and frustrating failures into a life of impeccable confidence and brilliant performance by simply changing your dominant thoughts. You must think on paper. Write down the following thoughts:

1. I am the architect of my destiny.
2. Thought by thought, I am changing my life for the better.
3. I am giving up my "blame game," which is an exercise in futility and frustration.
4. Day by day, in every area of my life, I am making progress.
5. I am giving 100% of my efforts to whatever work I do today.
6. I begin my day with an appreciation and gratitude for what I have, and I retire at night saluting my Creator.

Thought-Making Process

Thoughts happen. We think generally without effort. They come to you and me, and many times, the intensity of our thoughts consumes our entire attention. Then we say we are lost in thought. When we emerge from that thinking phase, we will feel good or we will feel bad, depending on the quality of our thoughts. It is an accidental phase of thinking, as we did not plan that thinking. Most of the time, the intruding thoughts play havoc in our minds, and we start seeing pictures that haunt us day and night. We can erase the possibility of intruding thoughts by deliberately cultivating life-giving positive thoughts. When we think of good things in life, good things do happen. Expect the best, and you will get the best.

Thought Culture

Thought culture is just like agriculture. It is the art of deliberately cultivating thoughts in our minds. Those thoughts get rooted in the depths of your mind, and it can transform your character, and hence your life.

Chain of Thoughts

One thought can lead you to another thought, and it leads to a third thought and a network of thoughts. If you are not aware of your thoughts, you could get lost in those unruly thoughts for hours.

Sow a Thought ——— TSA
Produce a Speech
Trigger an Action
Form a Habit
Create Your Destiny

Whatever thoughts you entertained yesterday got rooted in your personality as you spoke about them and such speech resulted in a corresponding action, which, when repeated, formed your habit. Those habits over a period of time shaped your character. By deliberately changing your thoughts (with thought awareness), you change the oral expressions, and noble actions stemming from such noble parents, you become a noble person.

Thought—Father
Speech—Mother
Action—Offspring (Child)

How to Induce New Thoughts

You can deliberately create new thoughts by taking deliberate actions. It is said that a weak person gets drowned in the sea of thoughts (as his willpower is weak), whereas a strong person follows an action plan to induce new thoughts that will bring a feeling of harmony and peace to their mind.

Daily Action Plan

Morning:

As soon as you wake up in the morning, instead of reading a newspaper or opening your iPad, you read a verse from the holy books of the Bible, Quran, Bhagavad Gita, or Talmud. You may read a few pages from your favorite inspirational book. A few minutes, thus, you spend as soon as you wake up, will set the tone for the rest of the day.

Select a few expressions that inspire you to include them in your daily conversation, such as:

1. This too shall pass.
2. As above, so below
3. Be indifferent to evil.
4. May I help you?
5. I am grateful (several times).
6. With God, all things are possible.
7. This universe is a kind place.
8. Life is beautiful.
9. A good day's work
10. Gratitude must be the only attitude in life.

When you repeat these expressions in your daily conversation with your wife (husband), children, coworkers, or even the boss, without you knowing it, you set in motion a train of events that produce harmony in the universe. All the expressions you include must resonate with your transparent sincerity. Every word you utter will draw power from the emotion you pour into the word. Every word packed with your emotion, will become so powerful that it will invoke a similar emotion in the receiver's mind. This is how great orators influence their audience. The only and the best way to inspire you is to inspire others. The best way to learn is to teach.

Lunch Break:

During lunch break, along with lunch, you can read an inspiring book before getting back to work. It will recharge you in the afternoon, and keep you going till the end of the day.

In the Car:

You can listen to some good, soothing music while driving home. Even better, you can listen to some inspiring audio tape so that by the time you reach home, you don't feel like a piece of log, but one full of energy. Your family does not want to see a drained husband and a deflated father. When you are upbeat at home, it can make a big difference in the home atmosphere too.

Watch Out for the Old Habits

The old habits have not left you completely. As uninvited guests, they are still lurking in the corridors of your mind. Beware of those inhabitants who could strike at the least expected moments. When they strike, have a defense mechanism put in place to defend your action plan. Make following your "mantra" to deal with the negative tyrants:

"I am grateful for this lesson."

At any cost, whatever you have to do, shun the following expressions:

1. I am tired (replace it with "I am terrific").
2. I am broke. (Thank you, Lord, for changing my situation.)
3. I am stupid. (My action was not wise; I need to be careful.)
4. I hate you. (Do not say anything; keep silent.)
5. It is over; I had it. (This too shall pass; I am grateful for the lesson.)
6. You are a pain in the "back." (I forgive myself and forgive you.)
7. Life is frustrating. (I shall overcome this experience.)
8. My kids are breaking my back. (I have growing pains too.)

At Night:

Before going to sleep, for a few minutes, be alone. Forgive yourself and forgive others if you think somebody's action left a negative impression on you. It will have a cleansing effect on the tablet of your mind. You are erasing from your mind those not-so-good impressions, so that they will not be rooted there forever. The mind is like a fertile field, and thoughts are spiritual seeds that can grow there, and the quality of the thoughts you consciously sow will help you build your character. If you sow the seeds of a thorn, a thorn will come out, and if you sow the seeds of delicious fruits, they alone will emerge. Everything that multiplies after its kind is a universal law, and it is invisible, like the law of electricity or the law of physics.

A prayer of gratitude is the best prayer to change your mind before going to sleep. A gratitude for another great day, expressing your appreciation for all the people, including the family members with whom you interacted during the day. Even if it was not an ideal day, still, you express your gratitude, as things could have been worse, but they did not. Always remember the following eye-opener:

"I had my blues
because I had no shoes

Until upon the street I saw
A man who had no feet." – *Author unknown*

The Art of Creation

Having understood the Science of Creation—which is nothing but transforming the unappropriated energy into an appropriated form of matter (condensed energy) based on the blue print of your desires—you are now ready to embark on a voyage of the Art of Creation. It is imperative that, you internalize the science of creation, before you start the practice of creative art. Everything you see is nothing but energy. You know energy cannot be created, nor can it be destroyed. It can only be transformed, with the agency of conscious mind. Willpower and thought power are synonyms, meaning one and the same thing. Just like a master craftsman is thorough with his tools, you, too, must be thoroughly familiar with the workings of the Tools of Transformation—Transforming thought energy into its physical counterpart.

Tools of Transformation

Your tools of transformation consist of the conscious mind and the subconscious mind. The dual functions of the mind made it necessary to classify them as two separate minds, each having a separate distinctive entity, for the purpose of understanding their unique roles in the science and art of creation. They are two partners, made for each other, and their partnership comes to an end when the physical body can no longer house them. A clear insight into the workings of the conscious mind and the subconscious mind is the key to utilizing the creative power within each of us to our best advantage. Most of us go through life without understanding the workings of our mind, often mismanaging it, to our dismay and disappointment. Then we blame everybody else for our failures and frustration, resulting in our inability to reach goals, whatever they may be. The power of the mind cannot be understated, as it is the cause of all our achievements and failures. It can be well illustrated by the following story, taken from Hindu mythology:

> A thousand years ago, there lived and ruled a king who was indeed very powerful. But he was not satisfied with his fame and name. He wanted to be an emperor, ruling over all the kings. So he propitiated Lord Shiva, the Hindu God of Dissolution, with his devotion and penance. At last, Lord Shiva appeared before him and asked him to request any boon the king would like. The king said with utmost humility, "Lord, I am not satisfied with myself. I want to be the Emperor, and all the kings in the land must submit to my reign. For that, I need power, and indeed, the strongest man in the world, to lead my army, and such a commander must be at my beck and call day and night, ready to take orders from me."
>
> Lord Shiva smiled and said, "Oh! King, I am pleased with your spiritual penances, and I grant thy boon. But there is one condition. This most powerful creature in the universe must be kept busy day and night. If he is left without tasks, he could eat you alive."
>
> The king answered, "Lord, that is not a problem at all, as I will have tons of tasks for him for the rest of his life."
>
> Lord Shiva vanished, and a gigantic-looking creature with fire in his eyes appeared before the king.
>
> "Sir, I am ready to take your orders."
>
> The king was very pleased. He began to enjoy his newly acquired power, and the entire palace was echoing the king's enthusiasm and confidence. But as the weeks passed by, the king

> noticed that the superman was finishing the most difficult tasks in no time and demanding more work. What started as a boon began to become a curse, and the king even feared for his own life.
>
> This is the time a well-known saint was passing through the kingdom, and the king asked his prime minister to receive the holy man with great honors and bring him to the palace. The king threw a royal welcome to the saint, and after the ceremony, the king narrated his plight after receiving Lord Shiva's boon. The saint asked the superman to be brought to the palace. Escorted by royal bodyguards, the ten-foot tall gigantic creature stood in front of the king and the holy man.
>
> The saint looked at the superman and smiled. He told the king, "Please erect a very strong pole made of teakwood in the courtyard."
>
> "With pleasure," the king told.
>
> The strong pole was erected in front of the palace. Then the holy man asked the superman, "You go up and down the pole until asked to stop."

The human mind is that gigantic creature, and if not engaged fully, it can "eat us alive" too. The mind must have a tract to run on all the time, and with a clear direction, it is capable of making us stronger and more powerful than even an emperor.

CHAPTER III

Organization of the Human Mind

Every human being, regardless of his or her origins or upbringing, has been endowed with a marvelous and mysterious apparatus called the mind. It is working twenty-four hours a day, producing conditions, events, and experiences in each of our lives. These conditions are always taking shape in the mind. Your mind is always busy weaving your tomorrow, either a tomorrow of joy or of sorrow, depending upon the thoughts you entertain in your mind.

Your thoughts are the tools with which you work, and they are the only tools you have to shape your destiny. Your experience in the outer world only reveals what is lurking in the secret chambers of your very own mind. Your experience is a mere reflection of your thoughts.

For example, you look into the mirror, and you don't like the face you see. If you are a woman, you'll change your makeup and hairstyle to look better. If you are a man, you'll comb your hair, trim your mustache, or shave to look better. But you will not break the mirror because you know that the mirror is only reflecting the face you have. Similarly, your experience in life is a mirror reflecting your inner thoughts.

Our circumstances are merely a "looking glass," a mirror of reflection. But in our daily lives, without realizing what we are doing, we very often try to break the mirror. For example, if you are not very happy with your income, you start criticizing your employer, the job, your upbringing, and everybody else for your shortcomings. You criticize your boss, who makes more money, and you talk maliciously about the Chief Executive of a big corporation who makes a million dollars a year. They are not going to change your conditions, which are merely reflecting your thoughts. To change conditions, you have to change the causes—your thoughts. Blaming your poor economic condition is like blaming the mirror for your uncharming face. Think about it.

After you study this book, you will learn not to blame the mirror for your poor image. You will consciously start working with causes, instead of conditions.

Conscious Mind and Subconscious Mind

The great Hindu seers, who spent their lives in search of truth in uncovering the mysteries of the mind, and in realizing the truth that "Me and my Father are one," had used the analogy of an ocean to describe the human mind. An ocean is a massive body of water with a surface and impenetrable depths beneath it. So is the human mind.

The human mind, like an ocean, is all one but endowed with two entirely different functions.

The surface mind is also called the conscious mind, the objective mind, or the male aspect of the mind. The deeper mind is called the subconscious mind, the subjective mind, or the female aspect of the mind. We will use the terms *"conscious mind"* and *"subconscious mind"* throughout our discussion.

The Conscious Mind

Most of us use only the conscious mind in our day-to-day transactions with the outside world. We use the sense organs and the brain to gather information and process it. This is done by the conscious mind.

The conscious mind is the choosing mind, the directing mind. It acts like a "watchman" at the gate. It is the rational mind. It argues. It uses logical reasoning. In other words, it works on the basis of inductive reasoning. Inductive reasoning is a process by which we compare facts to arrive at common elements binding them. In fact, the comparison of facts is the basis of inductive reasoning.

The conscious mind is the faculty that is endowed with the power of discrimination. The major difference between man and beast is that while man is endowed with the power of discrimination (the faculty of the conscious mind), the beast is deprived of it. For example, a dog walks into your yard, and you chase him away. But tomorrow, it could again make its appearance on your lawn. You go to your neighbor's house, and not only was the neighbor discourteous, but he also insulted you. You will try not to visit that neighbor again until he apologizes. This is because of the power of discrimination, which springs from the faculty of memory.

The conscious mind can also be called the master mind, the mind that directs and gives orders to the subconscious mind. One of the important objectives of mental science is to train students to use the conscious mind as a vigilante or guardian angel at the gate of the mind. A perfect harmony between the conscious mind and the subconscious mind is necessary to lead a life of peace and tranquility.

The Subconscious Mind

A major purpose of this book is to make the reader aware of the powers of the subconscious mind and how they can be employed to work for you, to bring all the happiness, riches, and peace of mind that one's heart desires. Please read and reread the following pages very carefully so that you can awaken a sleeping giant within you to work for you, to fulfill your desires, and to translate all your dreams into material reality. It does not matter whether it is multiplying your income, buying the dream mansion, or occupying an exalted position in society; your subconscious mind can help you achieve that. Most of us go through life without ever recognizing this power that lies dormant in each one of us, regardless of our race, religion, color, or upbringing.

The subconscious mind is the obeying mind. It is subject to the command of the conscious mind. Therefore, it is also called the subjective mind or the passive mind. It does not argue; it simply obeys the commands given to it. In other words, it works on the basis of deductive reasoning. Deductive reasoning presumes that the factors presented are true and proceeds to arrive at a conclusion without verifying the truth or falsity of any statements. It will work out the results as though the assumptions or suppositions are true.

The Law of the Subconscious

The law of the subconscious is the law of belief. The Great Master of Mental Science said, "Whatsoever ye shall pray and ask for, believe ye have received, ye shall receive." He was clearly commenting on the stupendous power of the subconscious mind.

Since the subconscious mind does not argue, as it does not compare facts, it will believe anything that is impressed upon it. It is like a sponge. It will absorb anything and proceed to make it a reality. Hence, we have to be extremely careful as to what we feed our subconscious mind and what thoughts we entertain in our conscious mind.

It is absolutely important to understand this particular characteristic of the subconscious mind. Let me explain it with another example. The subconscious mind can be compared to fertile soil. The soil simply receives whatever the farmer chooses to sow. It has only the power of acceptance and no power of rejection. Because it is an obeying mind, the slave and not the master, it is the passive mind.

It is up to the farmer to choose whether he wants to sow barley or wheat seeds. Similarly, it is up to your mind to select the thoughts (the seeds) to sow or drop in the subconscious mind (the fertile soil).

Amenable to Suggestion

The subconscious mind is always amenable to change by suggestion. Whatever the objective mind impresses upon it, with utmost perfection and fidelity, the subconscious mind reproduces and works out its final consequences. This is the basis of hypnotism. Under a trained hypnotist, the subject changes his personality for the time being; he believes whatsoever the hypnotist impresses upon him. There are instances in which the hypnotic effect has played the part of a great leader, an artist, a poet, or a writer with inimitable accuracy during the hypnotic state. Hypnotism cannot work, except under the law of belief.

Shakespeare said, "Assume a virtue if you have it not." He was really commenting on the power of the subconscious mind. Professor William James, the celebrated Harvard psychologist, advocated the "as though principle." Act as though you are happy, and you will be happy. Act as though you are successful, and you will be successful. Act as though you are rich, and rich you will become.

The American ingenuity that has presented mankind with such wonders as McDonald's fast food to flying palaces like jumbo jets has condensed this deep philosophy of mind into a few simple words: *"Fake it till you make it."* All of these great expressions point out the quality of amenability to change by suggestion possessed by the subconscious mind.

Autosuggestion

In hypnotism, the subconscious mind is under the command of a second person—the operator, the hypnotist. But the subjective mind, as it is called, can be subject to the command of your very own objective mind. Thus, when you consciously give carefully selected suggestions to the subconscious mind, it is called autosuggestion.

Autosuggestion is considered a very important training technique to change behavior patterns. It can even transform a person from a "sinner" to a "saint." Remember, the subconscious mind, without arguing, readily goes to work on whatever you impress upon it. A detailed discussion of autosuggestion and its benefits is the subject matter of a later chapter.

Actual Experience and Synthetic Experience

The subconscious does not know the difference between an actual experience and a synthetic experience.

For example, let us say that you were walking the streets of Calcutta during a recent visit to India.

The time was dusk, and the street was only dimly lit. You had heard before you left for India that the streets of Calcutta are infested with snakes. While walking, suddenly you stepped on something, and you felt it was a snake. You were shocked, and your body reacted in fear as though you had stepped on one. You immediately regained your composure, removed your flashlight from the bag, and realized the "thing" that you stepped on was in fact a piece of rope and not a snake. The fear and shock that enveloped your body suddenly vanished. But at that particular moment, the body reacted as though you had stepped on a real snake. This is because the subconscious does not know the difference between an actual experience and a stimulated or synthetic experience.

Imagination

It is said that imagination is the "workshop" of the subconscious mind. What you imagine, dream, or see before your mind's eye is going to appear as your experience, events, and circumstances. If you imagine yourself being successful, you will be successful. On the contrary, if you imagine yourself as a failure or a good-for-nothing person, your subconscious will definitely work hard to make your dreams come true. It simply obeys.

Therefore, mental science always warns you, the student, against dwelling on things you do not want in life. Instead, it advocates always dwelling on the things you want in life. Always dwell on health, wealth, prosperity, and peace of mind, and you will definitely be healthy, wealthy, prosperous, and at peace. The great Buddha imagined a world of peace and tranquility and entered into it. Therefore, it is said that we must think of only the things we want in life.

If you are a student and you want to get straight-A grades, only think of A's. Keep A before your mind all the time, dwell on A, and you will have nothing but A grades on all your tests. In other words, when you think of A all the time, you are cultivating A consciousness.

All human beings have a tendency to dwell on the negative; it is a natural tendency one has to consciously fight. When we want to be successful, we think of failure. When we want to acquire wealth, we think of poverty. We also criticize people who are wealthy and condemn the ways they acquire wealth. The great master said, "Yea, why look for the living among the dead?" He was pointing out the common fallacy of a man desiring happiness yet entertaining unhappy thoughts. You cannot go to a grave and look for the living because a grave is a resting place for the dead.

Look at this paradox in our own lives on a day-to-day basis. We want to be wealthy, yet we condemn wealth by criticizing people who have it. What we criticize stays away from us; what we praise is attracted to us. Then we complain that we are not becoming wealthy. It is like a man who wants to go east; he walks westward and complains that he did not reach the east.

Think about it. Keep your mind focused on the things you want. Do not dwell on things you do not want in life. Never look for the "living among the dead."

Builder of the Body

The subconscious mind is the builder of the body. It is a sleepless giant that controls the body twenty-four hours a day. Even when you are asleep, body functions like the heartbeat, digestive process, secretions, and excretions are going on without any interruptions. It is the subconscious mind that attends to each of these involuntary functions. The hair on your face and the nails on your fingers continue to grow, regardless of whether you are awake or asleep.

Perfect health is only a normal thing to expect, not an exception. The rhythm of the heart, lungs, and kidneys is actually thrown out of balance by our thoughts of fear, worry, and anxiety. So when you are upset about anything, the first thing to do is relax and talk to your subconscious about your true nature of perfect health and harmony. Believe that you are made in the image of God—that image is only of perfect health, harmony, and happiness. We must consciously implant thoughts of health and harmony into the subconscious.

Preservation of life is an eternal duty of the subconscious mind. The subconscious mind is pro-life, and its interference at any time is to save human beings from any impending dangers. The body has built-in mechanisms to remove any imbalance from its source. This task of keeping the body in harmony is the function of the subconscious mind. The subconscious mind knows what is good for the body, and anything in excess, whether it be sulfur, glucose, or any other chemical element, is discharged from the body involuntarily, without our conscious mind doing anything about it.

Trust your subconscious mind. Give it commands to restore you to perfect health; it will obey just like a faithful servant.

Subconscious at its Best

The suconscious mind is at its best when the conscious mind is in a state of abeyance. Bound to be so because the conscious mind is in a state of abeyance. It is bound to be so because the conscious mind is the arguing and rational mind, which questions every suggestion implanted in the mind. Therefore, it is suggested that the best results in impregnating the subconscious mind can be obtained in a sleepy or semi-waking state. A state of somnambulism is highly recommended for suggestion to the subconscious mind.

Look at the time prescribed for prayer by all religions in the world, whether Hinduism, Christianity, Buddhism, or Islam. Prayers are prescribed for dawn, midday, or dusk, which, in fact, are semi-waking hours when the conscious mind is in a state of abeyance.

This is exactly what a hypnotist does, too. The hypnotist relaxes the patient or person to be hypnotized before suggestions can be implanted in the subconscious mind of the subject (the person under hypnotism). There are instances in which the hypnotist fails to convince the subject, such as when the subject's own conscious mind refuses to be hypnotized. After all, hypnotism is a technique of implanting an idea in the subconscious mind of one person by another. When you try to impregnate your own subconscious mind through conscious efforts (with the help of your own objective mind or conscious mind), it is called autosuggestion. Autosuggestion is, in fact, a very effective technique for taming one's subconscious mind.

Extra-Sensory Perception

The subconscious mind is the seat of all paranormal functions like telepathy, clairvoyance, psychokinesis, out-of-body experience, etc. What we call paranormal, indeed, are the normal functions of the subconscious mind. Since the subconscious mind transcends time and space, it does not need the use of limited sense organs to gather information. It is extra-sensorial. All of us are endowed with the power of extra-sensory perception. Such powers remain dormant in us until activated by our own beliefs.

The celebrated mental scientist who wrote many books on mental science—namely Judge Thomas Troward—narrated an incident he and Mrs. Troward experienced while on a commission to India. Mrs. Troward, while stitching one night, was startled by a gunshot sound and saw a man who apparently shot himself dropping dead before her. The sound of that gun was also very clear to her ears. Later, Judge Troward, himself being a mental scientist, explained to his shocked wife this real incident that had taken place in the same room years before the Trowards moved to India. The suicide by the man who Mrs. Troward saw had left a psychomagnetic impression in the room. Any sensitive person could witness the incident, and Mrs. Troward being one, the vibrations in the room activated her subjective faculties, resulting in her perceiving the incident.

The subconscious mind operates in the eternal now. It has no past or future, as it works now. It is our rational mind that is conditioned by time and space. The memory of yesterday and a dream of tomorrow are both modifications of the objective mind. Beneath the depths of the subconscious lie infinite wisdom and endless possibilities. There is nothing hidden from the camera of the subconscious mind. As soon as you can activate this dormant power, events of the past, present, and future will unfold before your perception as a panorama of experience.

Thus, telepathy (mind-to-mind communication), clairvoyance (seeing into the future), psychokinesis (mind over matter), and spiritual healing are normal faculties of the subconscious mind. Since we are not aware of such powers hidden beneath our conscious mind, we call them paranormal functions. A major function of mental science is to bring home to every student the unlimited potential that waits for development and expression in our very selves.

The Yogis of India, though they attained all the occult powers (psychic powers), condemned those powers as obstacles to spiritual growth. Their contention was that such powers were distractions from spiritual practices whose sole motto is God-realization. As psychic centers were opened during their spiritual practices, the yogis began to experience various paranormal functions, which they ignored, paying no attention.

Points to Ponder

For understanding purposes, divide the human mind into:

1. Conscious mind
2. Subconscious mind

Conscious mind:

- The active mind, the objective mind
- It works on the basis of inductive reasoning (logical thinking).
- It is the master mind—the choosing mind.
- It is the watchman at the gate
- It gathers information with the help of the sense organs.

Subconscious mind:

- The passive mind, the subjective mind.
- It works on the basis of deductive reasoning.
- It follows the Law of Subconscious, the Law of Belief.
- It is amenable to suggestions.
- It is the builder of the body; it never sleeps.
- Paranormal activities are its "normal" ones—clairvoyance, telepathy, and such.

CHAPTER IV

Mental Attitudes

The old saying that "your attitude decides your altitude in life" is absolutely correct, and it really touches on the very core of mental science. The fundamental purpose of mental science is not only to educate the student on the workings of the human mind, but also to enable him or her to change mental attitudes to achieve whatever he or she desires in life. Scientifically speaking, it is the inner world of thoughts that get themselves translated into the outer world of events, conditions, and experiences. The loftier the thoughts we entertain, the nobler will be our experiences in life.

Thoughts are Things

An important principle of mental science is that all our worldly experiences, whether of joy or sorrow, stem from our very thoughts. So, we must check our thoughts all the time, and remove negative thoughts before they arise in our minds. But thoughts flash in our minds at a speed that exceeds lightning. Even before we want to stop thinking, thoughts have already come to pass. One way we can influence the quality of our thoughts is to eliminate negative speech from our tongues.

What you utter must always be positive.

As St. John said, "In the beginning there was the word, the word was with God, and the Word was God." The Vedas, the principal scriptures of the Hindus, the oldest will religion in the world, denotes "OM" (A+U+M) as a symbol of God, the eternal power that attends even to the minutest of life forms in the universe. Creation embodies three aspects of our everyday lives—thoughts, words, and deeds. If you cannot check your thoughts because of a lack of training in thought management, you can at least try to practice checking your words until you become proficient in managing thoughts. So, the student of mental science must always watch his or her words. What is negative must be eliminated at all times.

Let us take an example to understand the real importance of eliminating negative speech in our daily lives. Assume that you are talking negatively about a friend who has lost his job or has marital problems. When we talk about it, we are actually giving reality to these negative conditions, and not only that, by repeating that negative speech, we give reality to those negative conditions in our own lives. Through constant repetition, unknowingly, we tend to believe in those negative conditions, and slowly our beliefs will start producing similar conditions in our lives. This is why the great master said, "Be indifferent to evil," meaning you neither condone evil nor condemn it. Evil really means any thought that is not divine or godly. Think about it.

How to Eliminate Negative Thoughts

The first and foremost important thing to do to combat negative thoughts is to watch every word we utter. Every negative word we say or negative speech we produce blocks the flow of positive thinking and positive words. Infinite wisdom can flow to a person only through positive thoughts. When you constantly watch your words—the outcome of your thoughts—you are cultivating a positive consciousness or awareness, which, in turn, will facilitate the flow of infinite power toward you. The elimination of negative speech prepares your mind to receive infinite wisdom and all-knowing awareness. When the great master said, "I and my Father are one," he was referring to the close connection between the infinite wisdom, the seat of God, and the individual manifestation. Since there was not even a tint of negative thought in the son, he was the perfect conduit for the infinite intelligence to flow. When we are in definite agreement with the infinite thinking, like Jesus was, the infinite power will flow through us. In other words, our thoughts become the vehicle for the infinite intelligence to flow without any resistance.

Positive Self-Talk

A time-tested technique for the elimination of negative speech is positive self-talk. This technique can be well explained with an example. Metaphysicians and mental scientists from time immemorial have used the metaphors of darkness and light to refer to negative and positive speech, respectively. Darkness is really a condition caused by the absence of light. The moment you bring a candle into a dark room, the darkness is dispelled or removed. In the same way, when you always use positive words, there is no room for negative speech to thrive in your mind. Frequent self-talk of any positive nature will eventually saturate your mind, most importantly the subconscious mind, with positive infusion so that even the tendency for negative speech will be uprooted from the sphere of your mind.

Prayer—A Positive Self-Talk

Every prayer is in fact a positive self-talk—the lower self-talking to the higher self. All religions in the world promote prayer in one form or another. If you closely analyze prayer, no matter what religion it is from, it consists of positive attributes and praise of the Almighty. When you are praying and saturating the mind with positive attributes or qualities of the divine on a daily basis, there will be no room for the mushroom growth of negative thoughts. Prayer is the oldest and most effective technique for the elimination of negative speech.

What is prayer?

P—Positive Affirmations
R—Repetition
A—Attitude
Y—Yield
E—Emotions
R—Rebirth

Positive Affirmations

We start the prayer with positive affirmations like the thousand attributes or qualities of God, such as mercy, compassion, love, and forgiveness. The lead singer in a prayer group starts the prayer and is followed by the members of the group singing the hymns together. These positive affirmations form the basis of a thorough mental cleansing of the negative tendencies in thought, words, and deeds.

Repetition

Repetition, it is said, is the mother of perfection. Even when we are learning a skill, we repeat the technique several times to acquire mastery over the skill. This is true of a tennis player, a surgeon, or a piano player. Practice makes a person perfect in the skill practiced. When you repeat positive affirmations, you are saturating the subconscious mind with positive tendencies, which, in time to come, will be translated into their material equivalent. Thus, when you repeat the glory of God in a prayer, you unknowingly manifest those qualities in you, thus becoming a godly person.

A Negative Person

Repetition is a double-edged sword, meaning it works on a positive as well as a negative side. If you repeat thoughts of a negative nature, saturating the subconscious mind, they produce negative experiences, bringing your command to its true conclusion. Please remember that the subconscious mind is amenable to change by suggestion and that it is an obedient servant bringing forth its master's command to the right conclusion. A negative person is one who, knowingly or unknowingly, repeats negative speech and thereby "negativizes" the subconscious sphere. This is the secret behind "the rich getting richer, and the poor getting poorer." It is all in our thoughts.

Attitude

A prayerful attitude is always one of receipt. The devotee always prays for happiness and peace with a positive attitude, which thereby facilitates the timely realization of the objects of prayer. The great master said, "Whatsoever ye shall pray and ask for, believe ye have received, ye shall receive." This is also the secret behind people receiving what they pray for. The stronger the attitude of receipt, the more one will see crystal clear the objects of prayer before one's mind's eye as a present possibility. A positive attitude toward receipt is a prerequisite for effective visualization.

Do Something to Cement Belief

In order to cement your belief about the actualization of the visualized prayer, do something about it. In my earlier days of toying with the principles of mental science, I practiced this very thing. In 1986, at the beginning of the year, I wanted to own a Mercedes Benz car. I started visualizing about getting the car, and to cement my belief, I went to the hardware store and bought a key chain with a

Mercedes emblem. In less than six months, a Mercedes car came into my ownership from a very unexpected source.

If you are planning to buy a house, for example, at least buy a painting that you will keep in your living room. You have to keep on visualizing and also do something to cement your belief. The subconscious mind does not know the difference between a synthetic experience and an actual experience. This principle of the subconscious mind is effectively used by NASA in training astronauts who practice on earth in "simulated environments" in every aspect of their trip in orbit. After simulated training, the astronauts have no problem coping with conditions in space, as they have practiced them on earth before takeoff.

Yield

During the prayer time, the mind of the devotee or participant yields to the higher power, the Supreme Self, or the Omnipotent. Such total surrender or yielding is not possible unless the person has recognized the presence of such a power in the universe. When any person recognizes such a higher self and yields to that higher self, naturally, he will transform himself, if not fully, at least partially, to that higher consciousness. Prayer, as a technique, really helps everybody to be in tune with one's higher self or universal consciousness.

Emotion

Emotion is the fuel that drives people to a state of higher consciousness. The subconscious mind is the seat of emotions. As a matter of fact, any idea emotionally presented to the subconscious mind becomes easily absorbed by it and is sooner translated into its material equivalent. We see people weep and cry during prayer, with tears profusely trickling down their cheeks. The power of the spoken word is derived from the emotion with which it is said. An emotionally charged word is sharper than a sword, and it will come back with the result intended, either knowingly or unknowingly.

Any suggestion you want the subconscious to soon act upon should be made with emotional fervor. It is the eternal glue that sticks any suggestion to the subconscious mind. The reason why some people's prayers are answered sooner, while others wait forever and give up in frustration, is the presence or lack of emotion. As the intensity of emotion advances, the effectiveness of the prayer becomes certain without any doubt.

Rebirth

After a person has gone through the practice of prayer, the art of communicating with the subconscious mind, he or she becomes so relaxed and contented as if being reborn. The mental state has been transformed from tense to relaxed during prayer. The best way to forget one's worries or anxieties is to participate in any kind of prayer. It will help to calm the mind, and that calmness through repetition becomes a habit that slowly, through practice, will be woven into one's character.

Prayer, in short, is a thought management technique. It gives the individual who practices prayer a fresh mind, cleansed of all its tension. After praying, one feels the calmness that Mother Earth feels after a heavy rain—the impurities are washed away with a smell of freshness in the air. Such a mind is ready for creative thinking and constructive undertakings.

In both societies, oriental and occidental, all auspicious occasions begin only after prayer. It is a custom from time immemorial because our forefathers discovered that the secret of success in any human endeavor is prayer. The monotony and the flowing music really calm the human mind, like a lullaby lulls an infant to sleep. The agitations and the prattling of a busy day need to be calmed down for the conscious mind to find its restful state. Once the conscious mind is laid in a dormant state in a relaxed mood, the subconscious mind is ready to receive any suggestion without interference from the conscious mind. This, in short, is the secret of answered prayers.

Power of the Spoken Word

Words derive their power from the emotion with which they are uttered; hence the explanation for how a curse works. Ancient Rishis in India used to curse when they were angry and similarly offer boons when they were pleased. Both the curse and the boon were the direct effects of the emotion with which the words were uttered, as those saints had fully developed the faculties of the subconscious mind.

Jesus himself had cursed a fig tree to be barren, and it became so. The power of the spoken word must be realized by all of us in the modern age, as we indulge in destructive criticisms of other people. Any student of mental science must learn to eliminate negative speech from his or her vocabulary if he or she wants to cultivate positive thinking. Just like darkness and light cannot coexist, negative and positive speech cannot coexist. Therefore, it is imperative that one remove negative speech with vigilance and relentless practice. The following story will shed further light on this idea.

Certain creatures complained to the Sun that there was a very thick, dark spot in this universe. The creatures were frightened at the very thought of that spot. The Sun God said, "I have never heard of such a black spot in this universe, and I would like to see that spot." Followed by the creatures, the Sun went to that pitch-dark spot in the universe. The creatures were surprised to see that the dark spot vanished without a trace in the presence of the sun.

We must carry our own sunlight of positive thoughts and words with us, and we will no longer encounter the dark conditions of despair, despondency, and disappointment in our lives.

Watch Your Words

The words we speak represent our innermost thoughts lurking in the secret chambers of our mysterious mind. Therefore, it is imperative for us to check the words that come out of our lips. When you speak negatively, you create a negative world, and when you speak positively, you create a positive world. The choice of words we use in our everyday lives determines the quality of his lives. "Set a watch, O Lord! Before my mouth: close the door of my lips," said the psalmist. Every one of us must be vigilant at the door of our lips. We must consciously watch the words we speak under all circumstances.

The first step toward thought management is checking our spoken words. Thoughts travel in a flash, and we may not be able to control them initially. But we all can control our words, and that which is negative should not be uttered. We slowly get control over our thoughts once we start having control over the spoken word.

Unfortunately, the world has turned very negative; there is a lot of negative speech going on all around us. It is extremely difficult to be a positive person unless you work very hard all the time. We must stay away from conversations of a negative nature if we want to attain peace and harmony. We indulge in loose conversation about someone getting fired, another friend being sick, and someone else losing his or her business. When such talk continues, and if it is emotionally dealt with or without our knowledge, we are giving form and substance to such negative conditions in our own lives. The subconscious mind just obeys. It works on deductive reasoning. It does not differentiate between fact and fiction. "My master (conscious mind) is talking about sickness. Maybe he wants to be sick." This is how the subconscious mind thinks. The Biblical saying, "What I have feared has fallen upon me," is based on the premise that the passive mind is an obedient servant, bringing in our life sorrow as well as joy depending on what we talk about all the time. So, at all costs, we must eliminate negative speech if we are to get control over our thoughts.

How to Deal with Negative Experiences

Once we learn to eliminate negative speech, we are on our way to the royal road to a positive attitude. What happens in our everyday lives is immaterial, but how we handle it and with what attitude we receive it is the key to transformation. An optimist always looks for a ray of hope even in the worst of circumstances, whereas a pessimist always sees an undesirable thing even in the best of circumstances. The glass is always half full for the optimist, whereas it is half empty for the pessimist, though it is the same amount of water.

Common Negatives	How to Make Them Positive
1. I lost my job. What to do now?	I am changing my job. God has a better plan for me.
2. I am sick.	My body needs rest. I must change my living and thinking habits.
3. My wife is divorcing me.	My wife needs a change. I wish her the best in everything she does.
4. I lost money on bad investments.	I have learned the hard way on how to invest my money.
5. My business is bad.	My business needs more attention before it starts picking up.
6. My husband cheated on me. I shall teach him a lesson.	My husband needs help to get out of his temptation.
7. My boss is a jerk.	My boss has different challenges. Let me help him in any way I can.
8. I hate him (her).	I do not like his particular action.
9. What a lousy day.	The day just started. It will change for the better.

10. Why me, God? Look at all my troubles coming one after another.	I have problems. But they are opportunities in disguise.
11. I've had it. I'm quitting.	This, too, shall pass.
12. Oh, what a trial!	God, you are testing me, but with your help, I will come out clean.
13. Damn it! Why did I do it?	I am only human. Let me correct my mistakes and move on.
14. I will teach him (her) a lesson.	I forgive him (her) totally.
15. My parents are crazy. They want me to live according to the old ways.	My parents always desire my well-being. Let me examine their ways to find traces of old wisdom.
16. I overwork. Still, I cannot pay my bills.	I work very hard. I know that luck favors those who work hard.
17. I've lost all hope. Let me end my life.	I am riding through a stormy sea. Let me change the course for a better life.
18. It was my last hope. I don't know what to do.	God opens seven doors for every door closed.
19. This medicine is killing me.	Let me mix this medicine with a higher dose of prayer.
20. I am depressed. Nothing excites me.	Let me pray for more strength and vitality.
21. Those fears are haunting me day and night.	When God is with me, who can be against me?
22. I think I will fail.	With God, all things are possible.

23. I am buried in debt. I have no hope of a way out.	God is the source of all supplies. Let me tap that source for a way out.
24. I am dying.	"Day by day, in every way, I am getting better and better and better." (Repeat this 1,000 times a day.)
25. You don't understand me. I hate you.	Let me try to understand you, because I love you.
26. My wife does not respect me.	Respect is a two-way street. Let me show my respect to my wife.
27. My husband is an alcoholic. I cannot stand him.	My husband has a drinking problem. I want to help him get out of it.
28. I hate my job.	Oh, Lord! Guide me to a better job. In the meantime, let me give 100% to my present job.
29. I am a failure in life.	I found ways that wouldn't work. But let me keep trying new ways.
30. I don't care. It is your problem.	You have a problem. Let us work on it together.
31. My wife is nagging me.	My wife craves my attention. Let me spend more time with her.
32. My children drive me nuts.	My children need my help. Oh, Lord! Make me the best mother in the world by being all things to my loving little ones.

33. My wife called me a bad name.	My wife could not control her emotions. Please forgive me for my wrongdoing that threw her out of balance.
34. My husband called me a bad name.	My husband has a lot of pressure at work. Let me help him manage his stress.
35. This house is a living hell.	We have emotions running high here. Let us pray together for peace.
36. My mother-in-law owns my husband. She is possessive.	Just as I love my son, my mother-in-law loves her son (my husband).
37. I hate my mother-in-law.	I love my mother-in-law because she gave birth to my loving husband.
38. My wife always listens to her father. She doesn't listen to me.	Just like my daughter loves me, my wife loves her father.
39. I hate school. Let me drop out.	This semester was not the best. But let me try for straight A's next semester.
40. My family breaks my back.	My purpose in life is my family. Let me give them my best.
41. I hate to pay alimony to my ex-wife.	Let me reward my ex-wife for the good times we shared.
42. My ex-husband ruined my life.	I made a bad choice. Let me forgive my husband and change the course of my life.

CHAPTER V

Discovering Your Mental Make-Up

Every individual, regardless of race, color, or religion, is guided by innate tendencies, or *gunas*. The three *gunas* that pervade the universe are *sattva, rajas*, and *tamas. Sattva* represents purity, *rajas*, action, and *tamas*, inertia or dullness. The human mind, at any given time, is a combination of *sattva, rajas*, and *tamas*. Except in the case of a rarely exalted spiritual state of bliss, no person is exclusively sattvic.

Sattvic Mind

Sattvic mind can be compared to a mirror with not even a speck of dust on it. Such a clear mind alone can reflect the self or atman, according to Vedanta. A purified mind devoid of all impurities, reflecting the true nature of the self, can experience the bliss of salvation or freedom from the trammels of the flesh.

Rajasic Mind

The innate nature of rajas is action. Because the rajasic mind is engaged in numerous activities, the mental energy is fragmented thither and hither as if a mirror is tossed all around by a wind. A mirror constantly moving cannot reflect the true image of the self, though occasionally it gets a glimpse of it.

Tamasic Mind

The tamasic mind is totally immersed in tamas, or darkness, which is incapable of reflection except at the occasional prompting of the rajasic or sattvic tendency. It can be compared to a mirror covered by mud.

The following questionnaires will enable us to ascertain our predominant mental make-up. No purification of the mind is possible unless we know our mental make-up. If *sattva guna* is predominant, we call it *Sattva—Guna—Pradhana*; *Rajo—Guna—Pradhana* if rajas is predominant; and *Tamo—Guna—Pradhana* if tamas is the predominant tendency.

Mental Science: Mental Make-Up Test

The following quiz is divided into three sections. For the first ten questions, which apply to *sattva guna*, read each question and answer yes or no. For every question you answer yes give one point, giving a total of ten points each to *sattva*, *rajas*, and *tamas*. When you have finished, you will have three separate scores, one each for *sattva*, *rajas*, and *tamas*.

Section 1—Sattva	Yes	No
1. I often cry when I watch a touching scene in a movie.		

2. I become very unhappy when I hear about the personal problems of other people.		
3. I enjoy solitude, a sunrise, or a sunset.		
4. I prefer a fresh supply of fruits and vegetables over meat or fish.		
5. I have no problem tolerating people who do not agree with me.		
6. I prefer teaching at Sunday school over reading the Sunday newspaper.		
7. I forgive others easily for their shortcomings.		
8. I look at correcting my own weaknesses before criticizing others.		
9. I am always intrigued by the mysterious nature of human existence.		
10. In my life, people come first before anything else.		
Section 2—Rajas	Yes	No
1. I enjoy football games and other sports, and regularly watch them on TV.		
2. I love red meat, spicy food, and exotic dishes, and my meal is incomplete without them.		
3. I coach our community's little league baseball team.		
4. When I am right, I will argue until I win my point.		
5. I go to church (or temple or synagogue) only to please my wife (or husband).		
6. My favorite books are detective stories and adventures.		
7. I become tense as the deadline for my project approaches.		

8. My associates and subordinates cannot stand my temper.		
9. I become impatient and irritated if I wait for something.		
10. I cannot stand people who are lazy or inactive.		
Section 3—Tamas	Yes	No
1. I have to have at least ten hours of sleep.		
2. I can go without a shower for a couple of days, and it will not bother me.		
3. I enjoyed eating yesterday's pizza.		
4. I can watch any program on TV for hours together. (I am a couch potato.)		
5. I go to work only because I have to pay my bills.		
6. When my wife (husband) and children have some problems, it does not bother me.		
7. I enjoy munching on something all the time.		
8. My only ambition in life is to take an early retirement.		
9. I look forward to weekends, and I hate weekdays.		
10. I cannot understand why people spend hours together reading.		

Guna Imbalance

A *guna* imbalance is caused by excess *rajas* or *tamas* in one's mind. Since *sattva* purifies one's mind, any excess amount of *sattva* leads to spiritual enlightenment. Such an exalted soul may be found lacking interest in worldly affairs, as such a person is constantly going in and out of a state of blissful experience.

Excess *Rajas*

Excess *rajas* can create a lot of passion and lust in the individual. The best way to neutralize excess *rajas* is to get involved in spiritual activities like prayer, meditation, *japa*, and *satvichara*. This will also help to alleviate the problems of uncontrolled anger, fear, and greed. Any person afflicted by excess rajasic energy should regulate their diet to include more fruits and vegetables, drink lots of water, and learn to observe silence. After the initial evaluation, if steps are taken to remedy the rajasic excess, many psychological problems that could result may be avoided. One could find oneself confronted with tensions at work, loss of income or job, and sickness as a result of rajasic *guna* imbalance.

Excess *Tamas*

Excess *tamas* results in a lot of inertia, lethargy, and ignorance. Since tamas symbolizes darkness or ignorance, such a person afflicted by tamasic imbalance exists at a level slightly above the animal kingdom.

Our Mental Make-Up

Our mental make-up is based on the sattvic, rajasic, and tamasic content of our thoughts. It is very difficult to see a person who is predominately sattvic, rajasic, or tamasic all the time. Most of us represent a combination of two or more tendencies at any given time. The predominant tendency prevailing at any time determines our quality of mind and thoughts at any given time. With conscious efforts, we all can change the texture of our minds from tamasic to rajasic, rajasic to sattvic, or vice versa. One of the main objectives of mental science is to help the reader consciously change the texture of his or her mind for the better.

Gunas or Tendencies

The three *gunas* that pervade the universe, as we saw, are *sattva*, *rajas*, and *tamas*. *Sattva* represents purity; *rajas*, action; and *tamas*, indifferent dullness. No mind is purely sattvic, rajasic, or tamasic, as no tendency can exist by itself. Our purpose in mind control is to purify the mind by increasing its sattvic content. Depending upon the predominant tendency, we call a person a sattvic person, a rajasic person, or a tamasic person.

Rajo—guna creates *vrittis* or prattling in the mind, just like a wind causes ripples on the surface of the water. Any action that proceeds from *rajo—guna* is mixed either with *sattva* or *tamas*. All noble actions are rajasic based on *sattva*. All mean actions find their basis in *tamas*.

Characteristics of a Sattvic Person

1. A sattvic person upholds virtues, even at the cost of losing material possessions.
   (Examples are Mahatma Gandhi and Mother Teresa.)
2. He or she is involved in noble activities of charity and welfare for others.
3. Such a person devotes time and regularly to spiritual enlightenment like prayer, meditation, and austerities.
4. He or she observes silence and talks ill of none and good of everyone.
5. Such a person spends time in the company of like-minded holy persons or holy books.
6. His (her) actions are always based on love for others.
7. Such a person enjoys a purified mind and is on his (her) way to spiritual unfoldment.

Characteristics of a Rajasic Person

1. The word "*rajasic*" evolved out of the word "*raja*," meaning "king," who, in ancient times, was very active in the affairs of the state, including the protection of his subjects, which involves wars.
2. A rajasic person is always propelled by a desire for action. He is an active person, never found to be idle.
3. Such a person could be rajasic—sattvic, performing noble activities for the welfare of others; or rajasic—tamasic, engaged in activities of a lower nature.
4. In modern times, a rajasic person is found to be involved in sports activities, coaching, and social and spiritual activities in the community.
5. A rajasic person enjoys spicy food, exotic food and drinks, and an environment conducive to rajasic activities. A "sports fan" is a typical example of a rajasic person.
6. An excess amount of passion and lust is also a typical characteristic of a rajasic person.
7. Love for action makes a rajasic person very impatient at all times.

Characteristics of a Tamasic Person

1. "*Tamasic*" originated from the Sanskrit word "*tamas*," meaning darkness or ignorance, and as such, a tamasic person has a tendency to be sleepy and dull.
2. He or she is happy to be doing nothing and enjoys a state of lethargy.
3. A typical example of a tamasic person is a "couch potato," in modern times.
4. Such a person thrives on leftover food and stale food, and induces "*tamas*" through excessive eating.
5. Laziness also accounts for a tamasic person being careless, "unclean," and dirty.

6. Intellectual activities do not attract tamasic persons, and they like to engage in monotonous and routine activities.
7. They enjoy darkness or foul weather when the sun does not shine, so they could be indoors either sleeping or doing nothing.

Spark of Divinity

There is a spark of divinity in all human beings. The mind is created by *sattva*, and years of accumulated habits and tendencies brought from previous lives could cloud the existence of that spark of divinity. A clear understanding of the three *gunas*, like *sattva*, *rajas*, and *tamas*, and a determination to purify the mind through conscious efforts can transform even an extremely "tamasic" person into a spiritually promising "sattvic person."

> "In the beginning, when you are rajasic (passionate), you show the bitterest feelings or spite and revenge towards your enemies. As you advance in spirituality by selfless service and meditation, those feelings of hatred soften down gradually to simple indifference only. Later on, when you advance a step further when your mind if filled with mere 'sattva' (purity), even this indifference vanishes. You will develop intense love for them. You will develop pure equal vision." (Sama Drishti)

One can reduce the rajasic and tamasic content of the mind by consciously increasing the sattvic tendencies. An awareness at all times of the dire need to increase the sattvic thoughts is the first step towards such transformation. Anybody, regardless of his or her present circumstances, through sheer hard work and constant vigilance, can become a sattvic person. Do not blame your birth, upbringing, color of the skin, or education for your inability to be a better person. As a true Son of God, demand your divine heritage and become a sattvic person who, alone, is heir-apparent to the "Kingdom of Heaven."

How to Become a Sattvic Person

The following steps, regularly followed and incorporated into the daily routine, can make anyone a sattvic person in a matter of six to twelve months.

Food

You are what you eat. The contents of the food that you eat can favorably or unfavorably affect the content of your character. As Swami Sivananda said, "*Jaisa unn vaisa munn*"—"As is food, so is the mind." Food impacts tremendous influence on the mind of a person. We can learn our lessons from natural laws by closely observing Mother Nature. For example, a lion eats fresh meat and is a ferocious beast capable of killing even an elephant ten or twenty times bigger than the lion. But a cow, which merely exists on grass and herbs (not chemically fed), is a humble animal producing milk, which is second only to a mother's milk. There is a lot of passion, lust, and excitement in a person who thrives on nothing but red meat and spicy food rich in rajas.

1. Sattvic Food

1. Fresh food, like whole grains, wheat, rice, etc., and natural food with the least amount of preservatives.
2. Fresh fruits and vegetables.
3. Pure water, clarified butter, and milk.
4. All kinds of healthy food—freshly picked from the fields of Mother Nature.

2. Sattvic Emotions

1. Love—feeling that spirit alone is flowing
2. Compassion—the eternal urge to help and heal.
3. Forgiveness—the wisdom that God alone is perfect and all others have "weakness of the mortal."
4. Humility—feeling as humble as a blade of grass.

3. Sattvic Books

1. Bible, Gita, Koran, Talmud, and other scriptural books.
2. Epic stories from the Old Testament, Koran, Ramayana, and Mahabharata.
3. Biographies of great souls.
4. Inspiring books—ancient and modern.

4. Sattvic Thoughts

1. When God is with me, who could be against me?
2. With God, all things are possible.
3. *Allah dayat karo* (Allah, have mercy on me).
4. *Amme narayana* (Mother, my god).
5. The experience of truth alone results in freedom.
6. God is my master, my guide, my best friend, and my counsel.
7. Happiness is a habit; it can be cultivated by making small attempts daily.
8. Life is a sum total of small things that make a big difference.
9. Peace of mind is more precious than all the gold in the world.
10. The secret of happiness lies in making others happy.

5. Sattvic Acts

1. Be kind and tolerant toward others.
2. Refrain from gossip and speak ill of none.

3. Respect all people, regardless of who they are.
4. In times of trial, go into silence and search for answers.
5. Take responsibility for all your actions, good as well as bad.
6. Consciously avoid negative speech.
7. Understand that there is joy in giving. No one has become a pauper because of generosity.
8. Nobody will and can hurt you, if you trust in their divine nature.
9. Listen carefully to all; speak very slowly.
10. Take time for everything (as Swami Chinmayananda* used to say, "A place for everything, everything in its place").

An Ideal Day Producing Sattvic Current

Wake-up time: Before sunrise

First act of the day: As soon as you wake up, look at the picture of your favorite God (be it Jesus, Buddha, Krishna, or Siva). If there is no personal God you believe in, look at anything that reminds you of the Almighty according to your faith. Acknowledge your gratitude for another day in life.

Hygienic needs: Bathroom routine, answering bodily demands, brushing teeth, etc. During this monotonous task, sing a song, invite good thoughts, or review the exciting things you are going to do during the day.

Breakfast: Have a healthy breakfast according to your taste. During breakfast, read a passage from the Bible, Koran, Gita, or another holy book. Also review your short-term and long-term goals.

Note: In the morning, before leaving home, make sure you say good-bye to your wife, husband, or children and express your love. Do not quarrel with anyone before you leave home.

In Transit: While in transit to your place of work, listen to a preselected tape of inspiration, music, etc. When you are in the car, think good of other drivers on the road, even if they are not very nice to you.

At Work: As Sri Sathya Sabi Baba always says, "Help ever, hurt never" must be your guiding principle at the workplace. There is no substitute for being nice under any circumstances. Always avoid negative speeches at work, and do not collaborate with negative people.

Even if your boss fires you, keep your composure and say, "Thank you very much." Maybe the good Lord has a better plan for you, and your boss is only obeying the divine command from the Lord. Remember, a sandalwood tree profusely spreads its perfume even to those who destroy it by cutting its trunk.

Always be kind to people, especially those who occupy positions lower than you in the corporate hierarchy.

Back home: Do not bring your office problems home and cloud the peace at home. If you want to discuss certain things with your spouse or children, do it in a non-threatening way. It is a good practice to leave the problems of home at home and the problems of the office at the office.

Lunch and Dinner: Do not forget to eat food rich in sattva regularly. Drink plenty of water. Do not eat while walking or running. Take time to sit down and eat in peace.

Household chores: Spend time on household chores, helping your spouse and children. Listen to them carefully before speaking. Take a walk in the open air with your spouse or children. Watch a predetermined TV program with the family. If there is tension at home, stay calm. Keeping silent is the best remedy, until such time as normalcy returns.

Sleep time: Read an inspiring book such as the Bible before going to sleep. Never have an argument before going to sleep, nor watch a violent and disturbing movie before bedtime. Reciting a favorite "prayer" just before falling asleep is a very good technique for erasing your mind to a clean slate. Sleep by 10:00 p.m. or 10:30 p.m. unless there is a special reason, as you should not be sleeping late. "Early to bed and early to rise" is a healthy habit even for the twenty-first century.

Quiet time: It is a very good idea to have fifteen to thirty minutes of quiet time. This time can be used for mediation, reflection, or contemplation, or you could use this time for your prayer to your faith.

Mind Studying Mind

Mind studying the mind is the key to evolutionary progress. In other words, the mind, as an observer is looking at itself. It is reflection, contemplation, and meditation. You become a witness (*sakshi*) to everything that is going on within you, like a spectator watching a basketball game. But in reflection, the basketball player himself becomes the spectator. To quote Swami Vivekananda, the spiritual giant and beloved disciple of Sri Ramakrishna, "You work and think at the same time while a portion of your mind stands by and sees what you are thinking. The powers of the mind should be concentrated and turned back upon itself, and as the darkest places reveal their secrets before the penetrating rays of the sun, so will this concentrated mind penetrate its own innermost secrets."

Knowing your mental make-up using the questionnaire in this chapter will enable you not only to understand and manage your own mind but also that of others around you. An in-depth study of your mind and its tendencies will serve everyone as a valuable tool in the quest for happiness and harmony. Besides, it will promote greater understanding of other human beings with whom you interact on a day-to-day basis.

CHAPTER VI

Thought Management

Thought management is the greatest challenge that faces humanity today. It is a science as well as an art. Mental science offers a scientific basis for thought management. Yet, only through constant practice and application of various techniques can one become proficient in thought management. There has not been a comprehensive study on the subject of thought management. Even some of the techniques offered by various religious practices do not shed any light on the scientific aspect of the mind, thereby losing their appeal to the majority of educated masses. An attempt is made here to develop thought management as a valuable tool to guide our daily lives and improve the quality of our being. It is the author's hope that more and more attempts will be made to expand this area of mental science to enable people to unlock the door to their own inner world.

Techniques of Thought Management

1. Anchor Thought

The first and foremost technique of thought management is the "Anchor Thought Technique." Under this technique, there is a predominant thought to anchor the mind at all times. Ancient Hindu

Sages and their followers give to their disciples a *"mantra,"* or a sacred word, to recite all the time when the mind is not preoccupied.

The old saying that "an idle mind is a devil's workshop" is a true statement. Whenever the mind is not occupied, it will entertain random, undivine thoughts, which could lead the thinker to his or her peril. But if the mind is anchored on a mantra, it will not stray. The vibrations of the holy word will have such a refreshing effect on the mind that it will remain calm and serene all the time.

According to one's mental make-up and religious beliefs, one can choose an anchor thought. It could be the name of the Lord or a short hymn to Him, who pervades everything in the universe.

The following are some anchor thoughts one can follow in daily life:

1. Amme Narayana! (Mother, My God)
2. Om! Namasivaya! (Om! Salutation to Siva!)
3. Hail, Mary!
4. Allah Daya Karo! (Allah, Have Mercy on Me!)
5. Budham Saranam Gachami
6. Sriram Jairam Jai Jai Ram
7. Hari Om!
8. Sairam

I use this technique while driving or when I am not preoccupied. It helps to keep the mind occupied, and it also prevents random thoughts from entering the mind. In the beginning, this technique may seem peculiar, as you are not accustomed to anything like it. But after a couple of weeks, you'll get used to it, and your mind will enjoy it. It will keep the mind focused and refreshed.

2. Tortoise Technique

It is said in the Bhagavad Gita, the Hindu Bible, that just like a tortoise withdraws all its limbs to its shell, a man of perfection withdraws all his senses and the mind to himself. Here, the mind represents thoughts, and we can draw our thoughts to focus on the third eye or the center spot between the eyebrows. The thought energy is no longer dissipated as it is focused on a focal spot, and it will refresh the mind.

The tortoise technique is also a good technique for relaxation. You lie down and consciously withdraw all the sense organs and the mind to focus on the third eye to get maximum relaxation. When thus relaxed, respiration slows down, enabling all the cells to attain maximum rest.

3. Bead Technique

In many religions, spiritual aspirants count the beads in a rosary, or "*japamala*." Every time you utter a holy word or mantra one time, you count one bead. The bead technique is also a method of settling the mind. Monotony is a stage in which the human mind is at rest. Great spiritual seekers keep on counting the beads day in and day out to focus their attention. In the beginning, it is a tough task to concentrate and coordinate the recitation and counting of the beads. As time goes on, one will get used to it, and bead counting will become easy.

4. Chanting

Group chanting or individual chanting of the thousand names of the Lord, or the Lord's prayer, can help us manage our thoughts. The lead singer is followed by a number of people in the prayer group. The air in such circumstances is filled with a lot of emotion, and the singers all feel an uplifting spirit unleashed by the vibration. It is a good idea to participate in such chanting to manage one's thoughts. Any person coming out of such a chanting prayer group has better control over his thoughts. The emotions coupled with the soothing music will lull the mind. Just like an infant after an active day sleeps to mom's lullaby, our mind will enter a dormant state of inactivity conducive to creating a freshness of untold proportions.

5. Reading Scriptures

Anyone who reads scriptures such as the Gita, Bible, Koran, or Ramayana will not only learn to manage their thoughts, but will also be directing their thoughts toward spiritual achievement. Everyone becomes the object of his or her thoughts. Reading scriptural truths will saturate the mind with divine feelings, which bring celestial harmony to the person doing it. All spiritual teachers advise their followers to read at least a few verses from the Bible, Gita, or Koran daily to keep their minds filled with godly thoughts.

Rather than starting the day by reading newspapers, which contain the most disturbing news, always keep holy books with you and read them regularly in the morning. The semi-waking hours are particularly auspicious for reading because the passive mind during those hours tends to be in a state of peak reception. That is the best time to impress it with holy thoughts or positive, loving thoughts.

6. Thought Observation Technique

Thought observation is probably the best technique for thought management. The process involves simply observing one's thoughts. We must let the mind wander wherever it wants to go, but keep following it with keen observation. The mind is like a monkey. It jumps from one object to another with sporadic speed, and this technique enables us to follow it in its tracks. The key is that you are aware of your thoughts, and, with practice, this awareness becomes sharper and sharper. In thought observation, it is imperative that you don't criticize thoughts. They may be noble thoughts or very crooked or lustful thoughts, depending on the character of the individual.

The best attitude for thought observation is what is called a "*sakshi*" attitude. "*Sakshi*" is a Sanskrit word meaning "witness." You observe your own thoughts as a witness, as though you are not involved in the whole process of thinking. Taming the mind becomes very easy when you take the "*sakshi*" attitude, as it sharpens the perceptive process resulting from concentration only on thoughts. However unruly the mind appears to be, as it runs restlessly after objects of thought, it becomes tamed with this technique of thought observation.

With practice, the restless mind becomes restful as it dwells on a few thoughts and finally rests on one favorite dominant thought. When the mind slows down, you can anchor it with a "*mantra*" or a holy word.

Meditation

Thought observation is a prelude to meditation. According to Pathanjali, the great exponent of yoga, "yogas chitta vritti nirodha," which means stopping the prattling of the mind, is yoga. When you observe your own thoughts, the mind is looking at itself; it is reflecting on itself, and hence, the meditative process is also called a reflective process. Our minds are, by nature, restless like a turbulent sea, whipping up high waves of emotions until they are tamed to calm down, stilling all those disturbing thoughts. When emotions run high and thoughts run amuck, even a calm person becomes a victim of anger or rage. But with constant and faithful practice of meditation and observing one's own thoughts, the habit of calmness is cultivated, and such persons become habitually in control of their emotions. The greatest human challenge is managing one's emotions, which cannot be achieved without managing our thoughts.

Master or Slave?

You can be either a master or a slave, depending on who controls your thoughts. As a master, you have absolute control over your thoughts, and you need not worry about uncontrollable thoughts. As a slave, anybody can control your state of mind, as you are easily influenced. A person who acts upon his own volition is a master of his own destiny and has the willpower developed enough to act under trying circumstances. A slave is one who always reacts to the actions of others and thereby becomes a floor mat for anybody to step over all the time. When you learn to manage your very thoughts, you also learn to manage your very emotions and retain control of your mind.

Take the approach that "nobody can insult me without my permission." For example, if somebody addresses you as an idiot or a fool, say, "Thank you very much." The person who insulted you expects you to react, but instead, you acted. You did not fall for his comment. You know who you are, and you have learned to control your emotions and are therefore ready to act without becoming a victim of somebody else's comments.

When you train your thoughts, you also learn to act rather than react. You and you alone must have full dominion over the state of your mind. Thus, the intruding thoughts, works, or deeds of others, will have absolutely no influence on you.

Habit

Habit is a merciless master. You look at any alcoholic or drug addict, and this statement is proved without a shadow of a doubt. An act repeated becomes a habit, as repetition is the mother of perfection. That which you repeat, you shall become. An alcoholic, if you trace his story, probably started drinking as a social drinker with one or two drinks. As time marched on and social interactions increased, two and three drinks became more, making him a total dependent on alcohol. And the habit, no matter what it is, enslaves every human being.

If you have to be a slave to a habit, become a slave to a good habit. Begin cultivating the habit of managing your thoughts. When you are in control of your thoughts, you begin to act habitually, thereby forgetting to react even under trying circumstances. Good habits practiced over a long time become a part of our character, and that is how transformation takes place. No spiritual transformation is possible without thought management, as thought is the basic building block of spirit.

The constant practice of any of the thought management techniques described above will enable you to attain mastery over emotions. It will also help to eradicate anxiety, worry, and fear. A man in control of his thoughts is said to be his own master. He builds his future, carves out his destiny, and marches forward to accomplish his mission in life, whatever it may be. He does not worry about his circumstances that are adverse to the fulfillment of his mission. By careful practice of thought management, he creates his own circumstances, and a man of perfection is indeed a creator of circumstances and not a creature of circumstances like the vast majority of other people.

Right thoughts, correct words, and purposeful action alone can help one attain mastery over oneself. The key is thought management.

Points to Ponder

Thought management is the key to self-mastery in life.
With constant practice, anybody can manage their thoughts.
Thought management techniques include:

1. anchor thought,
2. tortoise technique,
3. bead technique,
4. chanting,
5. scriptural reading, and
6. thought observation technique and mediation

When you act, you are a master; when you react, you become a slave or a floor mat.

Thought Power

Thought, as we have seen, is the basic building block of spirit. It is a dynamic force resulting from the vibrations of the psychic "*prana*," or pure energy or life force. *Prana* has tremendous power to influence the thinker and all others who receive such thought vibrations. Our world is a thought world, a world created by the thoughts of millions of people. Thoughts can make or break a life. Do not underestimate their power.

Effect of Food on Thoughts

The food we eat has a lot to do with the thoughts we produce in our minds. According to Hindu philosophy, food plays a dominant role in our mental make-up.

Sattvic Food and its Effects

Fresh fruits and vegetables, clarified butter, milk, and other wholesome foods fall in the category of sattvic food. The consumption of such food produces divine thoughts in us. Divine thoughts are those that create, build, and sustain life and are always conducive to producing harmony in the individual thinker and others around him. Such thoughts breed love, compassion, forgiveness, mercy, and similar godly attributes in an individual.

Rajasic Food and its Effects

Foods such as meat, poultry, and spicy foods whip up passion in the individual, and the resultant excitement causes action. People who frequently eat rajasic food are very active; they cannot help but get involved in a lot of activities. The sexual appetite of such individuals is found to be very high. The chemicals supplied by this type of food keep the nerves in a state of excitement all the time. The royal family, the protectors in ancient times who needed to be alert and active at all times, ate a lot of rajasic food.

Tamasic Food and its Effects

Tamasic food, such as leftovers and stale food, creates a state of inertia in the individual. People who eat tamasic food are dull and inactive, sleep a lot, and prefer to remain drowsy. They are unable to be active because the chemicals supplied by tamasic food make their nerves dull or keep them in a state of drowsiness. All intoxicants supply inertia to the individual.

If the food you eat is fresh and pure, it produces pure thoughts. A saint or godly person eats sattvic food and produces pure thoughts. Such a saint speaks with authority derived from pure thoughts and produces a deep and lasting impression on the people who hear him or her. Such individuals influence millions of people all over the world with their pure and divine thoughts.

Watch What You Eat

Now it is very clear that we must watch what we eat. Fresh fruits and vegetables, clarified butter, and such naturally pure foods must be included in our diet. Consumption of such natural foods will produce pure and uplifting thoughts on a continuous basis, bringing more harmony and peace into our daily lives. Always remember that a pure thought is sharper than a sword.

Anytime you eat rajasic food on a regular basis—food rich in spices, protein, rich red meat, and the like—you will produce a lot of energy in the body, resulting in excess passion. Those chemicals will propel you to action all the time. This will also explain why sometimes there is an uncontrollable sex drive in people who, otherwise, are very calm in nature. In moderation, rajasic food should be taken to check the excess passionate surges. As far as possible, one must avoid tamasic food, which is the cause of inertia and dullness. Eating such unhealthy food in the long run can also affect your well-being, as thoughts always determine the nature of one's health.

Thought World

We create our own thought world. It is like a spider making its web. For example, imagine you are looking at a picture of your wife or husband, and the memories take you back in time to when you first met your spouse. The first time that you dated or kissed her (or him), and those memorable days of courtship will unfold like a panorama of romance. That thought could take you to the day you got married, and of course, who can forget the days of the honeymoon? If you continue to think, if there is no interruption, you may very well remember the day your first child was born, and all dominant events surrounding your married life. You go through this panorama of life as memory unfolds, creating an unforgettable thought world.

According to Hindu philosophy, this world exists only in our mind (*Manomatram Jagat*). Every thought is a vibration on the mind stuff—that stuff of which every human mind is made. All such vibrations never perish as they are all recorded as if on a tape or CD. Every holy and noble thought sets in vibration every sympathetic mind—a mind tuned into the same vibration.

Like Attracts the Like

This is a supreme universal law. We are all constantly attracting to ourselves sympathetic thoughts based on our very nature. A person good at heart sends noble thoughts and receives similar thoughts from others. Thus, without our knowledge, we are constantly setting in motion great forces that could influence the entire universe. Hence, there is a supreme need to monitor our thoughts and to make sure that we only send out pure and uplifting ones.

A person who is constantly thinking about liquor will end up in a bar. This is because of the operation of the law of attraction. Similarly, a person who has noble thoughts of helping others will finally take up a career in social service or medicine where he or she gets an opportunity to serve mankind.

Choose Your Thoughts

Every day, we entertain millions of thoughts. There are many events that trigger thoughts. If you do not watch your thoughts—and especially, by conscious effort, choose them—you may end up with thoughts you would not want to have realized. Thought energy is very powerful. The channels of its flow determine the nature of such thought. Every person's destiny is carved out by the thoughts he or she entertains on a daily basis. A sinner could become a saint by carefully choosing the thoughts that in time, will be translated into actions of a similar kind. Thereby the person ultimately becomes the object of his or her thoughts.

It is said that Sage Valmiki, the author of the famous Hindu epic *Ramayana*, was a wayside robber, baring people of their valuables to make his living. One day, he happened to rob a saint. The saint said, "I will give all my possessions to you willingly, if you just answer one question."

Valmiki said he would do that one thing without hesitation. The saint asked him, "Do you know that you, alone, reap the consequences of this sin, not even your wife?"

Valmiki said he robbed to take care of his wife and children, and, as such, he expected them to share his sin. The saint asked Valmiki to go home and ask his wife whether she partook in the sin of her husband. Valmiki set out for his house, while the saint waited for the answer to his question.

After fifteen minutes, Valmiki returned with gloom written all over his face.

"What happened?" The saint inquired.

"She said," Valmiki narrated, "everyone is responsible for his or her action, and nobody, not even a wife, will share her husband's sin." It was a revelation for Valmiki, who fell at the feet of the saint, who accepted him as a disciple. The same robber, by choosing divine thoughts, became a great sage and finally wrote the great epic *Ramayana*, which stands out even today as a magnificent masterpiece, a divine book.

Choosing thoughts deliberately is the first step toward transformation, but the human mind has a tendency to travel along crooked routes. Unless thought culture is carefully cultivated through vigilance and discipline, we all will become victims of bad thoughts. Man makes his destiny through his own thinking and action. If one makes a plan to choose thoughts wisely, he can change the course of destiny. A person unerringly becomes what he thinks all day long.

The great master asked, "Why look for the living among the dead?" We all do the same thing without realizing it. Everyone is engaged in the pursuit of happiness. Still, most waking hours, we all entertain unhappy thoughts. We want to be healthy, yet we think about sickness. We all love to be wealthy, yet we criticize people with wealth.

What a paradox it is! It is like a person who, wanting to reach the East, walks toward the West and finally complains that he did not reach the East.

We must choose happy thoughts if we want to be happy; we must choose healthy thoughts if we want to be healthy; and we must choose wealthy thoughts if we want to be wealthy.

Influence on the Body

Our body, in fact, is an extension of our own mind. It represents our beliefs—strongly cultivated thoughts about ourselves. Medical science has now acknowledged that a patient with a hopeful outlook toward life recovers faster from a disease than one who is fretting and fuming and has nothing but complaints. Every cell is in communion with every thought. A thought of love, mercy, compassion, and forgiveness vibrates the cell to its full potential, whereas every thought of hatred, jealousy, and rage contracts the cell, causing it to be weak and vulnerable to numerous germs around it. A harmonious mind in balance is a prerequisite for a healthy, vibrant body.

We also notice that a person with an outburst of emotions develops stress, anxiety, and, at times, high blood pressure. The medical profession is aware of the strong body-mind connection and advises patients to calm their mind by practicing yoga, meditation, and similar mind-control techniques. Similarly, a person who has good control over his or her mind and speech will have a calm and serene look with a sweet voice and lustrous eyes.

Be a Creator

Man is made in the image of God, who intended him to be happy, healthy, prosperous, and at peace with himself. By gifting the in the conscious mind, the choosing mind of man, God has bestowed on man the power of creation. One can create his own circumstances by consciously choosing his thoughts. Circumstances only reveal to us our innermost thoughts, and, as James Allen put it, "It is only a looking glass." As a matter of fact, the outer world is nothing but a reflection of our inner world—the world of thoughts and feelings.

Man is not made to be a victim of circumstances. He certainly can influence and change his surroundings by changing his thought patterns. The right exertion can alter the course of destiny and make man the creator of his or her own circumstances.

The study of the life of Mahatma Gandhi is a strong example of man's ability to change himself and thereby influence or change his circumstances. Gandhi's triumph lay in his ability to change within himself, and with radical inner changes, he changed circumstances to drive the British away and free India from decades of colonialism and foreign rule. He struggled to change from within by choosing thoughts of non-violence (non-injury), and in the process, he changed not only the course of his destiny but the future of millions of people.

It is said in the Bible that if a person strikes you on the left cheek, show him the right cheek, too. During the recorded history of mankind, there was only one person who practiced this biblical teaching. That person was Gandhi, who was smitten on the left cheek by a South African train examiner who did not want Gandhi, a colored man, to be in the first-class compartment. Without hesitation, Gandhi showed his right cheek to the train examiner. This also brings out another principle: that violence cannot be stopped by violence. It can only be curbed by love, compassion, mercy, and forgiveness.

Develop Individuality

Through thought discipline, one can also develop individuality—the distinction based on convictions and living with principles. We must always watch for suggestions that could easily influence our behavioral patterns. This world is full of suggestions, and we are all vulnerable to them unless we are vigilant against their gradual attack. Our character is modified daily, without our knowledge, by association with others. A man of weaker mind is more vulnerable to the suggestions of others than a man of stronger mind and willpower.

Thought discipline and concentration can help you break into new frontiers of subconscious faculties. When thought energy is concentrated rather than dissipated by random useless thoughts, it opens doors to paranormal faculties such as clairvoyance, telepathy, psychokinesis, and clairaudience, which are hidden in the realm of our subconscious mind.

CHAPTER VII

Power of the Subconscious Mind

Carl Jung, the world-renowned psychologist, noted that the subconscious mind contains not only the knowledge an individual gained during his life, but also carries experiences from past lives. By learning to draw the power of the subconscious mind, one is able to achieve anything he or she wants in life, be it power, wealth, health, or happiness. All the great men and women of the world in the fields of art, science, literature, and government were ordinary people like you and me, except they had knowingly or unknowingly stumbled upon the power of the subconscious mind.

Dr. Thomas Hudson, the pioneer in the field of mental science, has made the following observations about the subconscious mind:

1. The subconscious mind transcends reason.
2. It is independent of induction.
3. Knowing the power of the subconscious mind enables us to tap this vast reservoir of power and thus demonstrate our true inheritance from the Father.

SUBCONSCIOUS = THE SEAT OF MEMORY

The subconscious is the seat of memory, the granary of all our thoughts and impressions. According to Hindu sages, mental impressions, or *samskaras*, are not confined to what one acquires during this life, but also expand to experiences from previous lives.

Thomas Edison, the great inventor of the incandescent light bulb, admitted that "ideas are in the air." But very few people appreciate the power of his vast storehouse of knowledge, and a very small minority knows how to draw this power at will. However, many of us, by accident, enter the realm of the subconscious, and such thoughts are realized immediately.

Very often, our negative thoughts are materialized without our being conscious of them, as such thoughts are generally emotionalized. Therefore, it is imperative that we be careful to emotionalize only those thoughts that we really want to see materialized in our lives. In other words, do not think of things that you do not want to see actualized.

One of the major attributes of the subconscious mind is that it is amenable to change by suggestion. Whatever suggestion we give to the passive mind it will accept and work on to get it materialized. It is like a sponge or blotting paper, and it absorbs every thought earnestly presented to it.

This is the very reason why someone else's opinion becomes your reality, as your subconscious readily accepts that suggestion without questioning it.

Your subconscious mind is an inlet into the universal mind. It transcends time and space; it is total awareness without the use of sense organs. Its power is unlimited, and anything that you want in life that is embedded in righteousness, the subconscious can help you achieve.

Subconscious Mind—Your Creative Partner

Our subconscious mind is our partner in creation. God has made man in His image and bestowed upon him the power of creation. There is a vital force all around us, of which everything that has ever been created has been made. A thousand years before Jesus Christ, the *Upanishads*, the earliest scriptures of India, explained the three aspects of God (the mind) in the principle of *Trimurthy*. Jesus talked about the Father, Son, and Holy Spirit to form the Holy Trinity. In mental science, we refer to the conscious and subconscious mind, which, when working in harmony with each other, can accomplish even seemingly impossible tasks for any person.

We must follow certain steps in creation:

1. The objective of creation should be good; it should be pro-life and not intended to hurt anyone.
2. The mental image of the very thing you want (the mold) must be very clear.
3. Obtain knowledge that you have the power to draw this vital force at will.
4. Have total faith in your creative power, without any doubt.
5. Do something to convince your subconscious mind that you believe that you have received creative power.

The subconscious mind is entrusted with the task of preservation of life. It is always pro-life. The more noble and altruistic the cause, the more the subconscious mind will cooperate and work with the conscious mind to achieve any purpose. In other words, the purer your desires, the faster will be their fruition.

History is filled with instances in which the subconscious mind came to the rescue of individuals who, faced with extreme danger, accomplished seemingly impossible things. Its power is available to us twenty-four hours a day, but we seldom call on its attention to aid us in our daily activities. The purpose of this book is to bring you to a realization of this power hidden in you and teach you simple methods of drawing upon it at will.

Burning Desire

A burning desire is the first and foremost step in the art of creation. You must feel for the very thing you want to create. The great artist Michelangelo was working for days in a row, without ceasing, in his solitary workshop. He was completely out of touch with the outside world. A friend came and asked him, "Why are you working in solitude for days on end?"

Michelangelo said, "My friend, art is a jealous mistress. She wants the whole of man."

Say to yourself, "This One Thing I Want Very Badly."

The depth of your passion for the very one thing you want is measured by the sacrifices you are willing to make. Anything you desire wholeheartedly, you can have in your life. But very often, most of us do not know what that one thing we want in life. There is always some divine dissatisfaction urging you to move on to bigger things in life. It is the same dissatisfaction that drove Columbus across the ocean to discover new land. It urged Thomas Edison, an insignificant train boy, to be an inventive wizard at all times. The same inner urge drove Henry Ford, an auto mechanic at forty, to be the richest man in the world at the age of sixty.

Desire is the First Law of Gain

That inner urge, that voice of silence that whispers from within, is our higher consciousness. Most of the great people in the world had very humble beginnings, but they were all, without exception, driven by this inner urge to move on to higher and better thoughts.

Let us say that you are looking for answers to many questions in life. You have had your share of disappointments and disillusionments and are ready to throw in the towel and call it quits, saying, "I've had it." Remember that you are only using less than 3% of your creative mind, that mysterious apparatus of perception, while the remaining 97% remains unused. This is the power of your subconscious mind. There is nothing in this world that the subconscious mind cannot get for you, be it fame, fortune, harmony, or happiness. All that you need to do is impress upon the subconscious mind that things you want in life.

The great master said,"Whatsoever ye shall pray and ask for, believe ye have received, ye shall receive."

You Have to Believe

In a certain village in northern India, there was a severe drought, and everything in nature seemed dry and lifeless. The villagers were in total agony, watching cattle and other livestock perish from starvation and thirst. Unable to handle the situation, the villagers decided to invoke Providence by having a "community prayer" in the center of the village. They thought that through group prayer they could please Varuna, the Lord of Rain.

The entire population began to assemble at the village center to petition in prayer to the Almighty for much-needed rain. One family consisting of a husband, wife, and their four-year-old daughter was getting ready to go to the prayer meeting. To everybody's astonishment, the four-year-old took an umbrella with her.

"Sheela, why do you need an umbrella?" Asked her mom.

"Of course, we need an umbrella because it is going to rain when we pray," said the little believer confidently. Her parents laughed but allowed her to take the umbrella with her. To everybody's surprise, during the prayer, the clouds burst, and it rained and flooded the plains as though heaven broke open the doors of the eternal ocean. The little girl cemented her belief by taking an umbrella with her. We all must cultivate her belief and then our prayers will be answered by Providence.

Visualization

Visualization is the key to all achievements in life. "Believe you have received" means to see your object of desire as a present possibility. You must see yourself before your mind's eye in possession of the object of your desire. Of all the divine attributes man is endowed with, the most godlike quality is imagination. Visualization is nothing but imagination in action. When you visualize the objects of your sincere desire, you are focusing your thought energy on them, thereby building a spiritual prototype in your subconscious mind. Those spiritual prototypes form the first basis of creation, and in due course, those will be translated into their material equivalents.

Make your mental images crystal clear and very vivid before your mind's eye, and pour emotion into them. Anything with emotion held before the mind's eye, without doubt, will have its actuality in due course. Visualization is a double-edged sword; it can actualize your fears, too. Therefore, do not dwell on your fears; and give them substance and form. "What I have feared has fallen upon me" is a true statement, which has its basis in the law of visualization.

Keep one thought in mind and see it actualized in the present before your inner eye. Do not entertain doubts during the practice of visualization. It will dissipate the thought energy you are trying to project onto the objects of desire. Thought energy is the most powerful energy in the universe. During visualization, you are trying to project thought energy onto the things you want. The more you hold on to those visualizations, the better and faster their materialization in the realm of matter will be.

Practical Steps for Effective Visualization

1. Sit down on a chair or cross-legged on the floor, like the Eastern custom. Take a few deep breaths and relax your entire body. It is a good idea to first have a shower or at least wash your face in cold water. This will calm your nerves and evenly distribute the energy in your body.

2. Close your eyes. Begin to project thoughts on the object of your desire. Have a clear picture of yourself in possession of the object. For example, imagine you want to own a luxury-model Lexus. Determine the color of the car and every minute detail you can think of. Now see yourself driving the car on your favorite highway. Imagine driving this car with your spouse or a friend in the front seat.
3. Practice this visualization seven times a day, and thank your higher potential for granting your wish.
4. This should continue until you are finally in possession of your desired object.

How to Tap Your Subconscious Mind

A vast majority of the inhabitants of this planet, you and I included, use only 3% to 5% of our potential, and the remaining 95% to 97% is submerged in the deeper layers of the human mind. The greatest achievers in the fields of art, science, or government discovered their inner potential either by design or by accident. They mastered the technique of tapping the power of the subconscious mind, and with this newly discovered power, they could translate their dreams into reality. They were all common people, but with an uncommon purpose for the fulfillment of which they sought the partnership of their own higher potential.

When you learn the principles of the subconscious mind and are familiar with its attributes or qualities, you learn to harness this indescribable powerhouse capable of accomplishing humanly impossible feats. This little-known power exerts undue influence on every facet of our lives, be it personal, family, social, or business.

The subconscious mind never sleeps, as it attends to your involuntary functions during your sleep. It is an obedient servant of the conscious mind, and without questioning the "master," it will make sure that the master's "wishes" are carried out with cunning accuracy. There is no dearth of power for this sleepless giant, as it transcends time and space in carrying out the master's orders. Because of the strict obedient nature of the subconscious mind, the conscious mind has to be very careful in choosing its thoughts, which, when constantly dwelled upon, become the command for the subconscious mind.

Power of Suggestion

Suggestion is the programming language of the subconscious mind. Any suggestion you give to the subconscious mind will be carried out in minute detail, as it has accepted it as true. If you have doubts, for any reason, after a suggestion is made, it won't be acted upon as the doubts give mixed signals to the subconscious mind. We are living in a world filled with suggestions, positive as well as negative, that govern our actions on a day-to-day basis. A positive suggestion is one that brings harmony and peace, and a negative suggestion is one that produces discomfort and despair in its turn. We are all entertaining hundreds of suggestions on a daily basis, and some of them impact us more than others. The receptivity of any suggestion by our subconscious mind is always based on the condition of the mind. When a person is agitated and in a turmoil, the condition is favorable to receive any negative suggestions. On the other hand, when one is in a positive or inspiring mood, such negative suggestions have little impact on the mind.

The key is to be aware all the time that you are vulnerable to suggestions, and wrong suggestions can bring forth undesirable results and vice versa. The conscious mind must act as a vigilante at the gate of the mind. No thought or suggestion is allowed to enter the mind without a thorough examination of its content as to desirability.

The Subconscious Mind—Fertile Soil

The subconscious mind can be compared to fertile soil, where any seed can take root and grow in abundance. It is also necessary for us to understand that the subconscious does not have the power of rejection. It will accept any suggestion given to it without questioning it and proceed to work it out as a reality in life. Therefore, the conscious mind always has to be alert to protect the subconscious mind from receiving unwanted suggestions or thoughts. The function of choice is the duty of the conscious mind, the master who commands its servant—the subconscious mind—to act upon those commands. Like an obedient servant, those commands, whether good or bad, will be acted upon by the subjective mind with precision and dexterity.

The Rich Become Richer and the Poor Become Poorer

We always complain about the economic system, that it favors the rich as they become richer and is prejudiced against the poor who become poorer. In fact, it is not the economic system, but the thought patterns, that decide economic prosperity or poverty. People who are born rich or who have amassed wealth always entertain thoughts of wealth, prosperity, and economic progress, because their suggestions are always pro-wealth; they accumulate more riches by attracting them into their lives. Poor people, on the contrary, shun the rich people and claim that the latter amassed their wealth in undesirable ways. What you criticize—it is a universal law—stays away from you, and what you praise becomes your companion. The Law of Attraction states that you will be attracting to yourself at any time events, conditions, and experiences that are in alignment with your innermost thoughts. Taking it one step further, it means that your life is nothing but a true reflection of your innermost thoughts.

If you want to be wealthy, saturate your subjective mind with thoughts of wealth and prosperity. Do not ridicule the wealthy or the means by which they have amassed wealth. Instead, by creating thoughts of wealth, you set in motion a train of action that will finally create conditions favorable to the accumulation of wealth and prosperity.

Thought is the only cause in life. Conditions, events, and experiences are nothing but effects. If you are not happy with the conditions of your life, don't blame the conditions. Examine the causes that brought forth those undesirable conditions. For example, when you look in the mirror, you see your reflection and perhaps you do not like the way your face appears in the mirror. So, if you are a man, you shave, trim your mustache, and comb your hair to gentlemanly look. If you are a woman, you change your hairstyle and put on makeup to look more attractive. Nobody breaks the mirror, blaming it for your poor appearance. But in real life, blaming your condition is like breaking the mirror because conditions truly reflect your inner thoughts. So, we must examine the thoughts lurking in the secret chambers of our minds and change them if we are to change our experiences in life. Please take time to carefully review and understand the following:

1. Thought is the only primary cause in the universe.
2. Effects (experiences) are only manifestations.
3. When the cause is removed from the effect, nothing remains.
4. Wealth is a condition caused by wealth consciousness.
5. Poverty is also a condition caused by poverty consciousness or thoughts.
6. Remove those thoughts (the cause), and poverty (the effect) vanishes.
7. Health is a condition caused by health consciousness or thoughts.
8. Sickness is a condition caused by sick thoughts (the cause). Remove sick thoughts and sickness (the effect) vanishes.

Disease means "not at ease" (dis-ease), that is, a disturbance has started in the realm of the mind. All the sickness we experience can be our consciousness. Unknowingly, we dwell on those negative thoughts, causing bodily discomfort.

Therefore, long before the actual manifestation of the disease with the appearance of symptoms, the disease has already started. It started with a single DNT (Disturbing Negative Thought) which, when dwelled upon, many times affects the health and functioning ability of the cell—the basic building material.

A healthy mind (where thoughts are well balanced) alone can build a healthy body, and a healthy body alone can sustain a healthy mind. Indeed, our bodies are nothing but extensions of our own minds. The mind is the sum total of our belief system. Whatever you believe is your reality, and nobody but you alone can change your belief system. If you think you are healthy eventually, you'll become healthy when the belief system is strong enough to sustain those thought patterns. On the contrary, if you think you are sick, even before you realize it, your belief system will make sure that those symptoms of sickness appear in your body.

Harnessing Your Subconscious Mind is the Only Effective System Known to Mankind that can Change Your Belief System

Law of Belief

The Law of Belief is the law of the subconscious mind. This is based on the basic and wonderful attribute of the subconscious mind that it is *amenable to control by suggestion*. Hence, suggestion is a powerful tool to harness our subconscious mind, and thereby change our belief system. We know that the power of suggestion stems from its ability to influence the subconscious mind, which is weaving our belief system. All the strong impressions going into our passive minds are the threads that weave our belief system. If impressions that we feed our subconscious mind are negative, we build a negative belief system, and, conversely, if impressions we feed are positive, we build a positive system. We hold the key in our grasp when we know that our belief system, woven with deep impressions on the subconscious mind, in fact, carves out our destiny. A careful examination of the impressions that we feed our subjective mind is absolutely necessary. This will help us to install a selective system with a view to choosing only those impressions that are conducive to harmony, peace, and happiness.

Since suggestion in our hands is a powerful tool, it becomes clear that we can choose our very own suggestions and feed them to the subconscious mind on a deliberate basis. This deliberate, conscious selection of the suggestions to feed the subconscious mind is called "auto-suggestion."

Auto-Suggestion

Auto-suggestion is the art of feeding chosen suggestions to the subconscious mind, with a view to changing our belief system. The practice of auto-suggestion as a daily discipline is the key to changing our belief system by altering our thought patterns.

Before you start practicing auto-suggestion, you must review the attributes of the subconscious mind.

The subconscious mind (subjective mind):

1. is amenable to suggestion.
2. works on the basis of deductive reasoning. (It does not argue or analyze its contents for merit or demerit.)
3. is the builder of the body.
4. never sleeps.
5. transcends time and space; it works extra-sensorially.
6. has paranormal faculties like clairvoyance, psychokinesis, and telepathy as its normal attributes.
7. is at its best when the conscious mind is in a state of abeyance.
8. is the seat of memory.

When you study the above attributes of the subconscious mind, you will know the logic behind the technique of auto-suggestion, which can be practiced with the ease and convenience of any learning skill.

Steps in Autosuggestion

Step No. 1

Procedure

Relax your body. Calm the mind. Focus your thoughts on natural scenery like a sunrise or sunset. Feel each part of your body and say, "I love each and every cell in my body," and feel it.

Reason

The conscious mind is made to slumber—a state of abeyance.

Result

The subconscious attains a peak alert stage—a state of receptivity to receive suggestions.

Best time—early morning, or just before going to sleep—a semi-waking state.

Step No. 2

Procedure

Read aloud your positive suggestion. Example: "I am healthy, and in harmony with the universe; I love my very self. Like Emile Coue, the master of suggestive art, day by day in every way I am getting healthier and healthier. Thank you, Lord."

Reason

The message will sink into the subconscious. It does not argue, and it readily accepts it and acts on it.

Result

You will realize your dream (health).

Step No. 3

Procedure

Picture yourself very healthy and vibrant, the way you would like the end result.

Reason

Visualization (seeing before your mind's eye) is the key. The subjective mind does not know the difference between an actual experience or an imagined experience.

Result

Belief in health begins to take firm roots in your personality.

Step No. 4

Procedure

Do something that you would love to do when you are very healthy; for example, you love to play tennis when you are very healthy. So, go ahead and buy a tennis racket.

Reason

This act will cement your belief.

Result

Your subconscious mind begins to restore your full and complete health.

Step No. 5

Procedure

Thank the Lord. "Oh, Lord, I thank thee for the perfect health I enjoy."

Reason

When you are grateful for the blessings you enjoy, more will come your way. The master said, "Ye, first seek the Kingdom of God and its righteousness." [Perfection is the Kingdom of God. Righteousness, right thinking, denotes a feeling of gratitude]; "Everything shall be added unto you."

Result

Gratitude will decorate your behavior.

Conclusion

Repeat the above five steps for sixty days at least because repetition is the mother of perfection. That which you repeat, you shall become. It takes that much time to weave the impression of perfect health into your subconscious mind.

There is no simple technique that can take the place of auto-suggestion in harnessing one's subjective mind.

A Close Relationship

The subconscious mind is very close to its master, the active mind, in its mood and tone of thought. The conscious mind thinks both deductively and inductively. But the subconscious can only work deductively, as it is the servant and not the master. The master must choose whatever he wants in life—good, bad, or both.

The mind always works on the basis of reasoning based on a syllogism. Syllogism theory assumes a major premise, a minor premise, and a conclusion.

Major premise: Every virtue is an asset.

Minor premise: Truth is a virtue.

Conclusion: Therefore, truth is an asset.

Whatever major premise your conscious mind assumes to be true, the subconscious mind simply follows it. If your basic premise is true, the conclusion must also be true, and if the basic premise is not true, the conclusion will be untrue. The conscious mind has to make sure that its basic premise is right in order to arrive at the right conclusion. The subconscious is not endowed with the power of logical thinking. We must be careful always to choose a major premise as a guidepost in our everyday lives. This can be cultivated through constant vigil and practice. Just as a farmer examines very carefully the seeds that he is going to sow in his field, so also, we must examine every major premise we are going to dwell upon very carefully.

Selection of a Major Premise

Thus, it is clear that the active mind's selection of a major premise on which to dwell is the key to transforming one's life. You are what you think. If you entertain good thoughts, good will always follow. If you have evil thoughts, evil things will materialize in your life. Therefore, the moral is: do not dwell on things you do not want to see realized in life.

"Satsang"

"*Satsang*" is a Sanskrit word meaning "holy company" or "company of the good or holy people." By constant *satsang*, even a sinner will become a saint by transformation. In the company of good and virtuous people, thoughts, words, and actions will be only of a divine nature, and thereby all the people in that company benefit. Good thoughts always produce good effects, and harmony prevails. Whenever *satsang* is not possible, due to various reasons, the second best thing is to keep the company of good books like the Bible, Gita, Koran, or any other inspiring book. Every day, at dawn, before the day begins, try to read a few pages from the holy book or inspiring book. Those virtuous thoughts that you feed to the conscious mind—and more importantly, to the subconscious mind—will have a lasting effect throughout the day. Such accumulations of good thoughts slowly create a storehouse of good "*samskaras*" (impressions), which eventually transform the individual. So "*satsang*" or holy company, is a good habit to acquire.

"Satvichara"

"*Satvichara*" in Sanskrit means good thought or virtuous thought. We know now that every thought is the basic building block of spirit. By consciously invoking good thoughts or "*satvichara*" in the mind, two things happen. First of all, good thoughts produce good speech and good deeds, or karmas, in the individual. Second, if your mind is filled with good thoughts or *satvichara*, there is no room for negative thoughts to enter your mind. Slowly, "thinking good" becomes second nature to you, like brushing your teeth in the morning, and you finally become a very positive individual. So, cultivating "*satvichara*" is the key to becoming a profoundly positive person.

Now we know why the selection of a major premise is very important in everyday life. It lays down the foundation for a positive mental attitude. It saturates the conscious mind—and more importantly, the subconscious mind, the sleeping giant within—with all creative and positive thoughts. Individuals who dwell only on things they want in life, such as health, happiness, and wealth, have no room for moody or negative thoughts. They carry sunshine with them wherever they go.

Every day brings new and unexpected challenges for all of us. It is a good idea to carry some *satvicharas* with us all the time. They will be useful to combat the forces of depression and despair caused by the day's unexpected turn of events.

The following is a list of one-liners all of us can use for daily living:

1. With God, all things are possible.
2. When God is with me, who could be against me?
3. Thank you, "Allah," for your mercy.
4. The Lord is my savior and my guide. With His guidance, I can face any hardship.
5. "Sri Ram, Jaya Ram, Jaya Jaya Ram."
6. "Buddham Saranam Gachami, Dharmam Saranam Gachami."
7. "Amme Narayana, Devi Narayana."
8. Hail, Mary.
9. Love thy neighbor as thyself.

These *satvicharas* recited continuously, will keep the mind away from vexations and worries. They will slowly change you to become a profoundly positive person. A profoundly positive person is one whose *samskaras* or impressions are thoroughly immersed in divine positive thoughts and whose confidence is never shaken regardless of the day's events, as he understands the working of the mind. He always feeds good and positive thoughts to his mind and reaps the fruits of his good karmas or deeds by constantly keeping his thoughts focused.

CHAPTER VIII

Autosuggestion—The Ultimate Secret of All Human Achievements

Autosuggestion is a technique available to mankind from time immemorial to induce the subconscious mind. Any external suggestion accepted by an individual knowingly (and most of the time unknowingly) becomes an autosuggestion. Autosuggestion is a powerful mind management technique because it has an innate capacity to induce the subconscious mind, that "sleeping giant" who attends to every minute function of the body (all the involuntary functions like respiration, digestion, balancing the chemicals in the body, etc.) during the waking and sleeping hours. It is, in fact, a sleepless giant endowed with stupendous power that, when summoned, can carry out any seemingly impossible task, and the word "impossibility" is not in its dictionary. The only known technique for summoning the power of the subconscious mind is autosuggestion. Almost all of us use this power without the knowledge that we are invoking the power of the subconscious mind. The thoughts we think in the conscious mind, with emotion and passion, seep into the subconscious mind, which executes them with cunning accuracy. Before we can embark on the power of the subconscious, we need to examine the organization of the human mind.

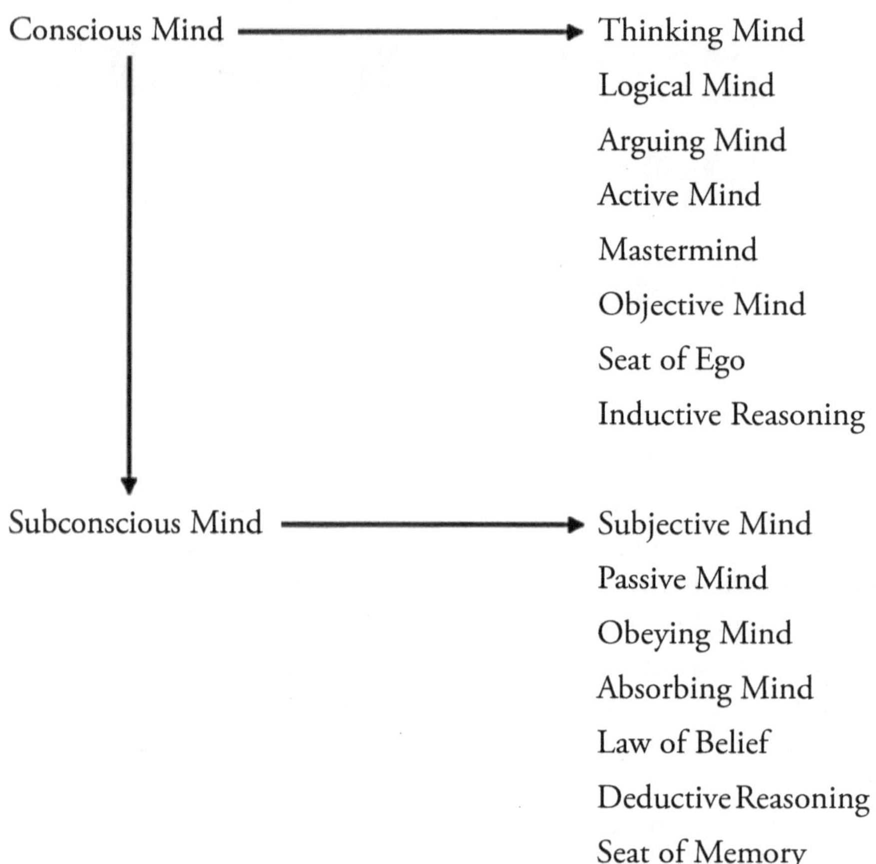

You have only one mind. Based on its fundamentally differing functions, it can be divided into the conscious mind and the subconscious mind. Each part of the mind is endowed with separate attributes and functions. The conscious mind is the directing mind and can be compared to the captain of the ship, whereas the subconscious can be compared to a loyal and willing servant of the master—the captain. The power of the subconscious mind is unfathomable, and it is also an inlet into the universal mind. Therefore, it can draw the necessary resources to carry out the master's orders from anywhere in the universe. The law of belief is the law of the subconscious. It is based on one of the outstanding attributes of the subconscious mind, namely that it works on deductive reasoning. It does not question the order given by the master. Therefore, it does not know the difference between an actual experience and a synthetic experience. Hence the saying, "Fake it till you make it."

"Whatsoever ye shall pray and ask for, believe ye have received, ye shall receive." This Biblical statement points out the Law of Belief, which is the Law of the Subconscious. Anything that you want to see manifest in life, see it as a present possibility. Visualize your desire as already fulfilled, and it will speed up its manifestation. Thus, your desires and dreams must be communicated to the subconscious mind through autosuggestion, and the subconscious will respond in kind by manifesting the desires that you impressed upon it in vivid details. The world without is nothing but a true replica of the world within. If you see disharmony in your life, you ought to go within to check the thoughts lurking in your secret chambers. They are one of disharmony and lack, and as you expel them from your mind, your outside condition will improve. Every thought lodged in your consciousness and accepted by the subconscious is a cause and it will germinate in time to give birth to the corresponding effect. So, if the effects (events, circumstances, and conditions) are not to your liking, you cannot change them unless you change the primary cause, which was the thought you planted in the soil of the subconscious.

Another analogy for the subconscious mind is fertile soil. Every thought is a seed you plant in the fertile soil of the subconscious mind, and it sprouts after its kind to produce the corresponding effect in the thinker. Just like a farmer carefully selects the seeds he wants to sow during the farming season, we all must be carefully selecting the thoughts we think and the words we speak as they seep into deeper layers of consciousness, where they are converted into events, conditions, and circumstances. As the great master of mind, Jesus Christ, said, "Ye shall know them, by their fruit." It means that from the experiences (fruit) you have in life, you can trace back the thoughts (the cause behind the experience).

Another outstanding attribute of the subjective mind is that it is amenable to suggestions. Every suggestion your conscious mind makes, or an external suggestion your conscious mind makes, or an external suggestion picked up by the subconscious when the conscious mind was in a state of abeyance, when accepted, becomes an autosuggestion. As we discussed before, the subconscious mind does not compare facts, and arrive at conclusions, as it is incapable of inductive reasoning. Therefore, it is imperative that the conscious mind must be "vigilant" at all times to make sure that no unwanted or negative thoughts trespass into the domain of the subconscious. To make the point clear, let us say that you have a new servant at home, who is not familiar with your relatives or friends. If anybody comes to your home in your absence (conscious mind is absent, because it is sleeping), and says he is your friend, the new servant will extend hospitality as though that person was indeed your friend.

This type of dangerous thought intrusion can take place, when you watch a violent movie, or read negative news after dinner late at night when the conscious mind is in a sleepy state. This is how people associating with negative people generally turn out to be very negative in their behavior. Therefore, it is very important for people to watch what they see, hear, or internalize, especially during those vulnerable hours of dawn, dusk, and midday. It is also equally important for parents to discriminate between positive and negative comments, as the children's innocent minds are like fertile soil, ready and willing to accept any seeds sown. Encouraging children to associate with friends who are positive and inspiring can also contribute to their healthy emotional growth.

Subconscious is the Obeying Mind

Since the nature of the subconscious mind is that of a loyal servant, it does not argue with the conscious mind—the captain of the ship. It does not talk back or compare facts, like the conscious mind.

The roles are clearly defined, and there is no gray area. This imposes a greater responsibility on the thinking mind. Thus, when you say, “I can’t do this,” “I am getting old,” or “I am broke,” you are causing harm and disarming the invincible power of the subconscious mind, which simply accepts your comments at face value, and moves the resources, necessary to carry out your orders. This is an all-the-more important reason for every person to be careful about what he or she thinks. Henry Ford, the famous industrialist and one of the richest men of all time, had an insight into the power of the subconscious mind when he said,

> “If you think you can do a thing, or think you can’t do a thing, you are right.”

You must think positively, you must speak inspiring words, and do non-hurting deeds all the time to get the maximum benefits from the invincible power of the subconscious mind. Anything you impress upon the subconscious mind by induced autosuggestion, will translate into its physical reality. The purer your intentions, the nobler your motives, and the sincerer your prayers, the manifestation will speed up itself, as there are no obstacles, impediments, or delays in your conscious mind. A total harmony between the two agencies of the human mind, is a prerequisite for success and happiness in everyday life. The wisdom of the subconscious mind is readily available to any person, regardless of his education, gender, color, religion, or race. Armed with the knowledge of the dual function of the mind, and recognizing the role of the conscious and subconscious mind, anybody can convert failure into success, poverty and lack into prosperity and abundance, and erase fear with hope and optimism. As the great mental scientist Emile Coue recommended, simply repeat the following suggestion in the form of a lullaby at dawn, dusk, or midday:

> “Every day in every way, I am getting better and better.”

First, chant this expression three times aloud so that you can hear it. The next three times, mutter it like a whisper so that your subconscious mind will be impressed. The third time, you say it mentally without moving your lips, and it will be woven into your character.

Your Conscious Mind—Your "Bodyguard"

Your conscious mind is, in fact, your bodyguard. The language you speak, and the thoughts you have are the protective armor around you. As the "captain of your soul," your thinking mind thinks only good thoughts, inspiring thoughts that you give rise to uplifting and equally inspiring words, which attract people of similar thoughts to you. When you have only love, compassion, and empathy for others, they, too, will reciprocate in kind—with similar thoughts and words. Since every dominant thought produces circumstances akin to its nature, it is impossible for a person of love and compassion to attract hatred and violence into his life. It is like a farmer sowing the seeds of oranges and getting a harvest of apples. Only oranges can come out of orange seeds, and only apples can come out of apple seeds.

"Circumstance is a Looking Glass"

As James Allen put it, "Circumstance is a looking glass." It means that you can look through the window of circumstance, to your secret chamber of thoughts and impressions. Your events, conditions, and circumstances in life are the offspring of your own thoughts, though they are seldom recognized by men. Just like the giant oak tree is slumbering in a tiny acorn, the mammoth wealth of a great industrialist hides in a simple idea he conceived and nurtured, and he has produced a product using that idea to change the way the world thinks. The Google and Facebook of today's digital era stand as indisputable testimony to the above truth.

Whatever you thought in the past made you who you are today, and whatever you think today will create your world of tomorrow. But it is tough and almost impossible for an ordinary person to break the old chain of thoughts, and he succumbs to his old ways of negativity and fear, blaming his fate for everything.

The power of spoken words is also echoed in the Bible, where it is said,

> "Death and life are in the power of the tongue, and those who love it will eat its fruit."
> (Proverbs 18:21)

If we examine our speech, it is nothing but a movement of spirit. The energy that is stored in us is expressed, and the expression results in speech. The origin of divinity was explained in the New Testament as follows:

> "In the beginning there was the word, and the word was with God, and the word was God."
> (John 1:1)

Thus, the word is the ultimate expression of spiritual energy. You can use electric power to light up the whole city, or you can electrocute as many as who touch a "live wire" hanging from a pole in the city. Similarly, you can uplift your conditions in life by using the positive tongue, from which only inspiration will roll out. You can also misuse the power of the spoken word (the expression of the ultimate spirit) by using your negative tongue, usually immersed in a pool of negative emotions like lack, poverty, judgment, hate, and rivalry.

Many people complain that they are used to negative expression due to their family background or other external influences. Of course, habit is a merciless master; it takes a Herculean task to completely get rid of it. Here, again, you can consciously choose words that you want to incorporate into your daily conversation. Read a few pages from your scriptures, like the Bible, Bhagavad Gita,

Koran, Talmud, etc., and underscore inspiring messages. Those messages invariably contain very inspiring positive words, which you will begin to incorporate into your daily conversation. You can also stop watching movies that contain vulgar language, especially at night, when the conscious mind may be slumbering. Another way to improve your positive vocabulary is to write down every day at least five inspiring words in the English language. An example is given below for ready reference:

> May I *help* you?
> I am indeed *grateful.*
> You are so *kind.*
> Your words are *inspiring.*
> I *trust* you.
> Your *faith* is *strong.*

The above exercise may appear to be small and simple. But there are no big things in life, but only small things that make a big difference. Just like the Chinese say, "A journey of a thousand miles begins with a single step." By taking these baby steps, you will learn to walk on the royal path of inspiration and optimism. A small dose of inspiration a day will provide the essential nutrients for your spirit and make you a strong person ready to meet the daily challenges.

How to Attract Wealth With Autosuggestion

"As above, so below
As within, so without."

The above words represent the ultimate secret of creation: the wisdom of the ancients, and the principle of manifestation. As above (in heaven, or spirit), so below (on earth, or in physical form). Thus, anything you want to manifest in your life, including wealth, must be borne out of a burning desire, a deep-rooted desire to manifest, possess, and enjoy every form of wealth. Such a desire can be created by consciously thinking about it until those thoughts become your dominant thoughts. Dominant thoughts attract similar thoughts, following the Law of "Attraction," capable of facilitating events, conditions, and experiences for the production of wealth.

"Mind is the Master—power
that molds and makes,
And Man is Mind, and evermore he takes,
The Tool of Thought, and, shaping what he wills,
Brings forth a thousand joys, a thousand ills -
He thinks in secret, and it comes to pass:
Environment is but his looking glass." - James Allen

Thoughts constitute mental energy, spiraling bits of electrons and protons moving at the speed of an electric train. But this energy has no form (unappropriated energy), and it has no direction. When you think about wealth, the word '*wealth*' followed. Your power of imagination started creating the spiritual prototypes of different forms of wealth, whether it be money, a home, an automobile, factory, or anything else. Thus, every form of wealth you see in this world is made by somebody's imagination—the most Godlike quality in man. There is a directing intelligence behind any form of matter, which is the condensation of pure energy.

In man, the directing intelligence is the conscious mind, the logical mind, and the master mind, which is the seat of the ego. As the Gospel of St. John explains, "In the beginning there was the word. And the word was with God. And the word was God." A word is the verbal expression of a thought image, which is the seed of every creation. Thus, every creation has to be preceded by a corresponding mental image. Just like a tiny seed of an acorn contains the potential of a gigantic oak tree, so also a small word "*wealth*" is filled with the potential to amass any kind of wealth in any amount. The word *wealth* represents potential wealth, which is anything of value that we want to possess. We human beings are endowed with this directing intelligence, known as the conscious mind. The degree of its development in each of us is based on the depth of belief in its power and its use to produce the wealth desired.

Intensity of Purpose

"Let there be light," commanded God—the creator, the architect of the universe. Since you are made in the image and likeness, you are endowed with the same power—the power of selection and choice. All of us use the power of creation and the power of selection in our everyday lives. But most of us are not happy and contented with the world we create. But we do possess the process of creation, and we are creating a world, but it does not appear to be a world of our liking. If the farmer does not like the harvest he got, he does not curse the harvest but, instead, changes the seeds he chooses to sow. Similarly, if we do not like our world—the effects of our thoughts—we must go back to our thoughts and change them. The subconscious acted upon your command (your thoughts) and created a world correspondent to those thoughts.

Alter Your Thoughts, Alter Your World

If you are poor, or do not have a well-paying job, or on public charities, you can change your poor conditions by altering your thoughts. This is a three-step process:

1. Write down your dominant thoughts.
2. Replace them with thoughts of wealth and abundance.
3. Change your friends and family if necessary.

Dominant Thoughts of a Poor Person

1. I am a victim of society.
2. Rich people and business people exploit the poor.

3. I don't have even a high school diploma.
4. I am not smart because I do not have a high school diploma.
5. I am a failure; it is my fate.
6. The government is not doing enough for us; we need more food stamps and more public aid.
7. America is doomed.

If you look at the above seven thoughts, there is one common thread binding all the thoughts. That is one of blame and lack of hope. There is also the absence of one common thought—personal responsibility.

No problem can be solved unless you take personal responsibility, for your current situation. It is also true that you cannot solve a problem, if your focus is on the problem. Instead, you think away from the problem—think about the solution. The more you think about the problem, more negativity will creep into your thought process, and the blame game begins, expending your energy. The subconscious mind, acting upon the master's command (the dominant negative thoughts), produces more of the same. And the problem becomes deeper and deeper, with no solution in sight. When someone asks you, you say, "The same old, same old..."

Replacing Thoughts—of Wealth and Abundance

1. I am grateful for the wealth I have.
2. I am grateful for the home we have.
3. I am grateful for the cars we have.
4. I am grateful for the freedom and peace I have with wealth.
5. I am grateful for the knowledge I have for creating wealth.
6. I am grateful for the wealth consciousness arising in me.
7. I am grateful for the awareness that wealth is good for the uplift of mankind.

Wealth-Creating Rituals

1. Release money with joy; it will come back to you multiplied.
2. Show respect towards any form of wealth—cash, checks, automobiles, homes, etc.—that represents wealth in its physical form.
3. Write checks with joy, even if they are for a parking ticket or a traffic ticket. (Affirm—I am grateful for the lesson.)
4. Show generosity in small matters (e.g., if you give a $2.00 tip for a personal service, increase it to $3.00, and $3.00 to $4.00, etc.).
5. Being wealthy is a "mindset," so always think of the good things money can do.
6. Avoid using the expressions "I am broke," "I have no money," etc. Instead, always remain grateful when talking about money, and dealing with any form of wealth.
7. Never think of taking advantage of another person, when you are negotiating to buy a home, a car, furniture, etc.
8. Always insist on the salesman making a reasonable commission for his services.
9. If you see a "homeless person," give him five or ten dollars with love. Never make any negative comments about his "predicament."
10. Wish for others, what you wish for yourself. (Do not feel envy towards anyone for their success and prosperity.)

If you look at wealthy individuals, they are the champions of charity. They use part of their wealth for the common good, to help the underprivileged and weaker sections of society. They set up endowments and scholarships in schools and other educational institutions. In short, they release money with joy, and it comes back multiplied.

The Greatest Charity

The Bill and Melinda Gates Foundation is one of the richest charities in the world. The foundation has assets worth over 75 billion dollars, and both Bill and Melinda are committed to making a positive change in the health and well-being of people, particularly in developing countries. They both travel to many countries and focus on prevent- ing needless deaths caused by a lack of vaccines and encouraging families to adopt contraceptives to limit the deaths of young women during childbirth. Their personal interaction with those underprivi- leged men, women, and children stands testimony to their personal commitment to change the world for the better. They are two caring individuals who want to share their wealth with the world, so that it will be a better place to live for millions of people who have no chance otherwise to improve their living conditions.

It is no accident that Bill Gates, the founder of Microsoft, is one of the richest men in the world, with assets worth over 75 billion dollars. If we all can learn one thing from the lives of Bill and Melinda Gates, it's that we all can make a difference by helping fellow human beings in their difficult situations to face the challenges of everyday life. You do not have to be a billionaire or even a millionaire to open your wallet for the needy brothers and sisters who share Planet Earth with you. You do not have to travel to third-world countries in Asia or Africa to extend a helping hand. You find opportunities in your own backyard, to help the local food pantry or the soup kitchen, which feeds the thousands who remain hungry otherwise. It is the birthright of every human being, wherever they are, to eat at least a couple of times a day, and it is the moral responsibility of every one of us to make sure that we pitch in to promote the cause.

As the New Testament states, "Whoever has will be given more and they will have an abundance." In the biblical story of the talents, those servants who doubled their talents for their master, were given more and invited to partake in the happiness of the master. And the one servant who did not do anything with the talent given to him, was punished, by taking away what was given to him. Wealth is something to be shared so that it can multiply, and that which is hoarded and withheld will eventually wither away. A part of your wealth (even if it is only a couple of dollars), must be set aside and given to charity, which can use it to take care of the needs of the underprivileged, poor, and hungry in the world.

The secret of increasing wealth by giving is enshrined in the very law of the universe:

"Universe reciprocates in kind—manifold."

Almost all the wealthy people know this secret, and they have all opened their wallets to support various humanitarian needs around the world. One of the richest men the world has ever seen, namely John D. Rockefeller, knew the secret of increasing wealth by giving at the very tender age of sixteen. Even though he was making a meager amount of fifty cents a day, he used to set aside a part of it for savings, and another part for charities. A sixteen-year-old boy, setting aside money for charities from his meager wages, only a John D. Rockefeller could have thought about such a noble act.

The Science of Getting Rich

The Science of Getting Rich is a classic in the field of new-age psychology and self-help literature, written by Wallace D. Wattles. He has extensively described in his book the spiritual aspect of material accomplishment, especially relating to the art of getting rich. The fundamental truths about getting rich are nothing but a paradigm shift, a mental make-up, an attitude of abundance in everything, and a rearrangement of one's thoughts mired in wealth consciousness. You can cultivate wealth consciousness by carefully choosing the thoughts that induce wealth and abundance in place of poverty and lack. Just like a farmer who decides to reap a harvest of wheat and carefully selects the healthy wheat seeds to sow in the prepared field, you, too, can select thoughts of abundance and wealth in the fertile soil of the subconscious mind. It is the receptive mind, and it acts on any command given by the conscious mind.

Tree of Abundance

Thoughts of abundance and wealth we consciously think about, and they become manifested in due course as wealth in different forms. Thinking thoughts and creating effects (of abundance or lack of it) are going on in every human mind. Most of us experience lack because our minds are constantly entertaining the fear of lack and limitation. The moment we change our thoughts, we are on the royal path of abundance and plenty. Rich people surround themselves with rich people and various forms of wealth; they engage in conversation with their friends about wealth production; and they release funds to make a difference in the lives of less fortunate ones. Their minds constantly swim in the ocean of wealth consciousness, and because they sow the seeds of wealth, they harvest wealth in different forms throughout their lives.

Wealth is Your Birthright

Wealth is your birthright. Demand it by first choosing thoughts of wealth and abundance. Surround yourself with people who are wealthy, or at least go to the library and read the biographies of Andrew Carnegie, J. P. Morgan, Henry Ford, John D. Rockefeller, Bill Gates, Warren Buffett, and other self-made billionaires who started their lives in humble surroundings. Their thoughts were soaring like an eagle, and they knew exactly what they wanted. Their thoughts were focused, and they backed it up with sheer hard work and ceaseless optimism. That does not mean that they did not face challenges; they did just like you and me, but their determination to succeed was too strong to be defeated by any undercurrents of adversity.

Think Big

Most of us settle for less and underestimate our potential. The following poem should awaken in us an urge to ask for more from life, who is a "just employer."

"I bargained with life for a penny
And life would pay no more,
However, I begged at evening
When I counted my scanty store.
For life is a just employer;
He gives you what you ask,
But once you have set the wages,
Why you must bear the task.
I worked for a menial's hire
Only to learn, dismayed,
That any wage I have asked of Life,
Life would have paid."
(Jessie B. Rittenhouse,
("The Door of Dreams")

How to Think Big?

This is a four-step process.

1	*Know what you want.* For example, I want a beautiful white brick home.
2	Formulate the thought of a beautiful white brick home.
3	Register and hold the thought in your mind. The best way to accomplish this is to see the picture of your beautiful white brick home with your inner eyes. (Mentally visualize the picture of your beautiful white brick home.)

4	Relax and let go. This step is a very important one to practice. When you relax and let go, you are not worrying about the way your desire is going to manifest. This is the time when negative thoughts could creep into your domain of consciousness. You will start doubting your ability to manifest your beautiful white brick home. If that happens, you simply state, "I am grateful for the lesson."

How I Manifested My White Brick Home

I personally went through the process in 1989, when I manifested my desire of having a beautiful two-story white brick house. Our old house was getting smaller as our three boys were growing bigger, and we started looking for a home. Since my wife wanted to live only in Elmhurst, we were looking for a house on the south side of Elmhurst. I was driving around on my way home one day and saw a beautiful house for sale on the south side of Elmhurst. I suddenly fell in love with the house, as it was a beautiful white brick home—two stories, of course. I told my wife, and we went to an open house that weekend. My wife also liked the house, as it had five bedrooms, 2.5 bathrooms, a big basement, and a big backyard for the kids to play.

There was only one problem: that we were planning to go to India the next week to celebrate my mother's 84th birthday. It is a big celebration in Indian culture, as a person is said to have seen one thousand full moons when she turns 84. We were all excited about the trip, and I told my wife that if it was meant for us, surely, we would have it.

The next few days, we remained in town, and I went on my ritual to drive around the house in the morning on my way to work and in the evening on my way back. Before we left for India, I must have driven around the house more than a dozen times, and the picture of this beautiful house was implanted in my inner consciousness. I visualized the home in minute detail, and especially the Italian marble in the foyer was a point of attraction for me. I was also thrilled to have a first-floor office room for myself with lots of book shelves to house my collection of books. With all the enchanting details in my mind, I was able to visualize the home day and night.

We went to India for six weeks and came back just in time for the school opening for the kids. The same day we landed in Chicago, I went to see the house from outside. I was slightly disappointed as the "For Sale" sign was gone. Maybe it was sold, I thought. But I was so attached to the house that I decided to call the owner whose telephone number I had. His name was Mr. Louis, and he told me that he did not get any reasonable offers, so he took it off the market. I really felt a sigh of relief and told him my interest in the house. He was also very happy that I was interested. After discussing with my wife, I met with Mr. Louis during the Labor Day weekend and made an offer he could not resist. He looked at his wife for consent, and she nodded, signaling her agreement, and he accepted my offer. There was no real estate agent involved in the transaction, which was the main reason why it was very attractive to the owners.

Even though I had similar experiences in the past, this was a major event involving our primary home. This experience only confirmed my belief that our desires are manifested first in the mental plane, and then they descend into the physical plane. My falling in love with the home at first sight was my spiritual acceptance of the home, and my constant visits and visualization expedited acceptance by the subconscious mind. Even though there was a gap of almost two months, my desire was so deep and emotionally charged for "my dream home" that the subconscious mind orchestrated all the events that led to the withdrawal of the home from the market by the owners. This is clear evidence that the power of the subconscious mind to carry out its command with cunning accuracy cannot be underestimated. When I left for India, I had no trace of fear in my mind that I might not get the house. I was confident in my mind that if this home was meant for us, nobody could take it away from us.

There was also another factor that led to the consummation of this real estate transaction. I did not take any unfair advantage of Mr. Louis' situation, as I offered a very reasonable price, which, coupled with the absence of any realtor, made his financial situation better by accepting my offer.

We also told the Louis family to take whatever appliances or other personal property he chose, and they were very grateful for our gesture of goodwill.

Obstacles to Wealth Accumulation

Let us look at Mother Nature. She is profoundly wealthy, and abundance is her calling card. Wherever we look, there is prosperity and wealth. Similarly, if we take mankind as a whole, collectively, we have immeasurable wealth; it is spread across all the seven continents, and as we progressed during the last one hundred years, we collectively accumulated more than our previous generations put together. Every generation becomes more aware of the need for wealth accumulation, and due to better economic conditions, they are able to put aside more than their previous generation.

1. Dominant Thoughts are Anti-Wealth Creations

Our thoughts are influenced by our family, society, teachers, and others who could have been directly or indirectly associated with our mental development. Many people misinterpret the scripture and say that money is the "root" of all evil. Scripture says that the love for money (to the exclusion of everything else) is the root of all evil. Money is, indeed good as long as it brings joy to others. But if you accumulate it only to hoard and not to give away to those in need, it could lead to evil thoughts and actions, which could lead to financial ruin.

Thus, if you have been misinformed about what Scripture says about money, that it is the root of all evils, now you can correctly interpret it to say that, "Money is good as long as it brings joy to others."

From today onwards, you will watch your thoughts to make sure that they are not anti-wealth accumulation. You can look at money as a means to an end—and it could be for food, clothing, or shelter. It could also be used to make positive changes in the lives of others. In your conversation with others, think positively about wealth in general and do not condemn any form of wealth. You must shun any negative thoughts or speech about anything in life. Any negativity, either in trait, behavior, or environment, when discussed and thus relived, will take strong roots in your consciousness and become a part of your own personality. Always remember that today's life is nothing but the harvest of yesterday's thoughts. If you do not like what you see in your life today, you will have to alter the thoughts that went into the making of today.

2. Negative Imagination

Another obstacle to wealth accumulation is the imagination of lack, poverty, and fear. Many of us are the victims of negative imagination, which is either genetically transferred or acquired from association with friends or family members who habitually think negatively. The aphorism "What I have feared has fallen upon me" is a very true statement, as it invites those fear thoughts to manifest as your experience in life. Every negative thought, as soon as it creeps up, can be converted into its positive counterpart.

For example, if you are afraid of losing your job, and your imagination paints the details of your fear and anxiety, just say loudly, "I am grateful for the lesson." If one of your associates at work got laid off, rather than talking about the employment policy of your employer, just comfort your associate by saying that "when one door closes, seven doors open." Maybe the good Lord has a better plan for you." Rather than leading a conversation stemming from negativity, you can lead your associate through an inspirational path of optimism and expectation. If you can send his resume to a few of your friends for consideration, that will be ideal. That is what being a good friend is all about.

3. Ignorance of the Source of Supply

The source of all wealth is spirit—unappropriated spirit. You are surrounded by a sea of unappropriated spirit, and God, the creator, your own higher potential, has given you the tools to convert the unappropriated spirit (energy) into appropriated energy in any form you choose to have. Thus, wealth in any of its forms is your fruit for asking once you know how to ask. "Ask, you shall receive; seek, you shall find. Knock, it shall be opened unto you." This is not a religious statement; it is, in fact, a metaphysical truth expressed in simple words.

You have to shake off the thoughts of lack, limitation, and poverty. Instead, fill your mind with thoughts of plenty, abundance, and wealth. Every thought is pregnant with an invisible power capable of transforming the unappropriated spirit into any form you choose to visualize. As explained in *The Science of Getting Rich:*

> "THOUGHT is the only power that can produce tangible riches from the formless substance. The stuff from which all things are made is a substance that thinks, and a thought of form in this substance produces the form."

Here, thought does not mean a random thought that flees the mind after a short visit. A strong thought, a dominating thought with fervent emotion, becomes a command to the subconscious mind to act and create a corresponding form, and it simply obeys the master.

"No thought of form can be impressed upon the original substance without causing the creation of the form."

"What Have You Got in the House?"

There was a multitude of crowd who followed Jesus for three days, and they were weary and tired as they had not eaten anything. The disciples were puzzled because they had hardly anything enough to feed the thousands of men, women, and children. "How many loaves have ye?" Jesus asked them. Jesus took those seven loaves and gave thanks and broke. Then He gave to the disciples to set them before the multitude to eat. There were a couple of pieces of fish too. And Jesus blessed that and commanded the disciples to put them before the people. All of them ate and were filled, leaving a few pieces in the basket.

In this miraculous feeding of the multitude, there hides a spiritual principle: "Anything you have, even if it is so little, if you bless it, and express your gratitude, it will swell and multiply." This is the Law of Increase.

You can apply this spiritual principle to your task of building wealth. Even if you have no significant amount of money, you express gratitude for what you have and bless that form of wealth. Release it with joy for a common good; it will come back to you multiplied. When you do this, have an unshaken faith in this principle and patiently wait, expressing gratitude for fortunes to materialize in your life.

The Law of Increase says:

"I am success, though hungry, cold, ill clad,
I wander for a while, I smile and say,
It is but for a time, I shall be glad
Tomorrow, for good fortune comes my way,
God is my Father, He has wealth untold,
His wealth is mine—health,
happiness and gold."
(Ella Wheeler Wilcox)

Whatever is praised and blessed, multiplies. This is the eternal law of increase. It does not matter what your financial situation is or how deeply in debt you are; if you practice this Law of Increasing Returns, you will invite good fortune into your life. Your emotional prayer will cause the unappropriated energy (this is the spiritual energy that belongs to none—a spiritual no man's land) to move, causing the formation of the wealth you desired.

It may not necessarily mean that somebody is going to transfer money into your bank account. Instead, a friend of yours could suggest you to apply for a position in his company, and the paycheck from that employer could be a direct transfer into your bank account. Opportunities, however miniscule they may appear to be, do not let them pass by.

Our advancement as the entire human race has taught us one very important lesson that nature obeys us in exact proportion to our own obedience to nature. This law is equally applicable to us in the field of building wealth. We need to respect wealth by obeying the principles of wealth creation, and we need no more worry about being wealthy as the flow of wealth towards us becomes imminent. When we study the lives of the richest people in the world, one thing is for sure—they all revere wealth; they adore wealth; and they use it for the benefit of mankind. In short, they release wealth with joy, and it surely comes back multiplied!

"Assume A Virtue, If You Have It Not" (Shakespeare)

This is a very wonderful mental science principle. You can very well use it to be rich. When you fill your mind with thoughts of wealth, you begin the journey towards riches. It is a single step any aspiring wealthy person can take. Register the thought of being rich and hold it in your mind until the message is picked up by the subconscious mind, which will act on it to convert your desire into a physical reality. You can take the following steps to assume the virtue of being rich:

1. Think Like a Rich Person

The first and foremost thing a rich person does is to revere and respect money. Do not throw a dollar bill like a piece of garbage. When you come home, if you have any change in your pocket, please put it in a coin jar and never throw it. Even the smallest denomination of a coin—like a penny—is representative of wealth. Even when you talk about money, say good things and remain grateful.

Similarly, when you write a check for any reason, release it with joy even if you are writing a check to the Internal Revenue Service or the State Department of Revenue. Anything you release with respect will come back to you and many times multiplied.

Another important characteristic of a rich person is that he honors his financial commitments and pays the bills on time. Paying your bills on time shows respect to the other person who has to fulfill his financial commitments with the funds you transfer. It is also true that a good percentage of your credit score (30-35%) is based on your on-time payment of your financial obligations. Such on-time payments will enhance your credit score, which is a barometer of credit worthiness in the lending world.

2. Dress Like a Rich Person

You do not have to go and buy a $600.00 or $1000.00 suit to dress like a rich person. Depending on your dress code at work, you wear clean clothes and iron them at home. Wearing good clothes also positively impacts your mental attitude. Your personal demeanor should be one of inspiring and uplifting rather than promoting a negative feeling of depression. It should never invoke sympathy in others.

3. Speak Like a Rich Person

"Richness" does not only mean material wealth; it also denotes spiritual wealth. The soothing and inspiring words you speak promote spiritual well-being in your friends and associates. The same tonality of voice you must use when talking to your spouse and children. Anybody can use an inspiring expression to feel good about himself or herself. The best way to stay inspired is by inspiring others.

4. Act Like a Rich Person

Most rich people are very humble, and humility is one of their outstanding personality traits. Especially when they are dealing with their personal staff, they show more compassion and empathy. Their wealth has not inflated their ego; rather, it has only made them very caring human beings. There are always exceptions to the general rule, and we are not talking about those exceptions. You act the way you want to act when you become rich.

If you think like a rich man, you speak like a rich man, you dress like a rich man, and you act like a rich man, you are already a rich man. You must be rich in your own mind first before you appear before the world as a rich and successful person.

CHAPTER IX

A Grateful Mental Attitude: Practical Questions.

Question 1

WHAT IS LIVING IN GRATITUDE?

Living in gratitude is remaining grateful day and night, regardless of whatever challenges one has to face. It is unconditional gratitude. Conditional gratitude, expects certain benefits to be received to be grateful. When a person remains grateful under all circumstances, he/she is unconditionally grateful.

Question 2

Do you mean to say that, I should be grateful even when 'bad things' happen? For example, my father just passed away? You are asking me to be grateful for this painful experience.

Yes. Father finished his mission and departed. Understand that his death is not the end of his life. It is the end of a life cycle. One cycle ends and another begins.

First of all, this is an appropriate time for you to express your gratitude to your departed dear father, for all that you have learned and inherited(spiritually)from him.

Second, the mind is rattling like a rattle snake as the incident temporarily deranged your mind. An ounce of gratitude introduces immediate sanity to your mind. Gratitude really speaking is the ultimate 'mind cleanser'. It removes in its entirety all the negativity. A mind devoid of negativity is fresh and creative, ready to take on any tasks. Third, with the onset of a new freshness, you can do a better job of consoling your mother, and your siblings to help them regain their composure, and peace of mind. After all life is all about taking care of others. You can be that 'anchor' your family just lost.

Question 3

How do I start living in gratitude?

Start the day with gratitude. As soon as you open your eyes in the morning, before leaving your bed say a prayer of gratitude.

"Oh! Almighty God, I am grateful for all the blessings I enjoy. I am also grateful for a great day, just beginning for me".

If you are religiously oriented, read a prayer of gratitude from your scripture – Bible, Gita, Quran or Talmud, or any other scripture.

Question 4

How do I continue the feeling of gratitude throughout the day? How can I remind myself of the need to be grateful? You can keep a pack of Love to do list. Keep reading them at regular intervals, and adding one more thing to be grateful.

Question 5

How do I end the day with gratitude?

Just before you retire for the night while in bed recite the following affirmation: "OH! ALMIGHTY GOD! I AM GRATEFUL FOR THE ABUNDANCE OF HEALTH, WEALTH, HAPPINESS AND KNOWLEDGE".

Repeat this affirmation like a 'lullaby' as your mind slips into peaceful sleep.

Question 6

I know gratitude is a great attitude. But how can I be grateful to people who try to hurt me at all times?

Gratitude, is not only a great attitude, it is an elixir of harmony. Gratitude must be the only attitude in life. When you show gratitude at all times, to everything and everybody, they too change because you change. Every circumstance you encounter is your own creation. When you think about the 'hurt' more and more, it sinks deeper into your subconscious mind. As it gets lodged in your subconscious mind, you will get more the 'sense of hurt', which you wanted to avoid in the first place. Hence it is written in the bible, "What I have feared, has fallen upon me".

Question 7

You said that gratitude must be the only attitude in life. How can I cultivate the gratitude, as a guiding principle to manage all my affairs?

It is indeed a very good question, though simple, is very profound and reaches the very philosophy of gratitude.

The secret of training the mind lies in understanding the harmony between the master mind (conscious mind) and the servant mind (subconscious mind). The master is the discriminating faculty of man. It is the thinking mind, the reasoning mind. It works on the basis of inductive reasoning. It compares the facts and arrive at logical conclusions.it is the rational mind. Our logical thinking is the very nature of Master Mind. It thinks like A=B, B=C, therefore A=C.

The servant mind, though by nature is the servant, it has access to all the power and resources in the universe. Yet it needs to be commanded to do whatever, you want to cultivate. By definition, being the obedient servant that it is, it simply obeys the command of the Master Mind.

In understanding the wisdom of the subconscious mind, and the power of the Master Mind to command the Servant Mind, and the techniques of doing so, is the key to supercharging your mind to peak performance.

The Subconscious mind, by definition, works on the following basis:

It works on deductive reasoning.

It is amenable to suggestion.

It transcends time and Space.

It is an inlet into universal mind, here every thought ever produced by any man is stored and kept.

The paranormal qualities, like clairvoyance, psychokinesis, telepathy are normal faculties of the subconscious mind.

It is the source of all power.

It absorbs anything that is impressed on it, it is like a sponge.

It is the builder of the body and the source of all healing, physical and emotional.

To cultivate the quality of gratitude, one is encouraged to use the affirmations, and the Tablet of Gratitude at regular intervals to impregnate the Subconscious Mind. When you recite the following affirmation,

"I AM GRATEFUL FOR THIS EXPERIENCE",

the subconscious mind, responds as follows:

"My master thinks, that he/she is grateful for this experience, let me make sure that he or she is right". So, all the experiences that follow will prove that the attitude of gratitude is created and maintained at all times.

So, the precision with which the subconscious mind works is amazing as it exceeds the talent of the brightest mind in any field.

Question 8

How can one say in all earnestness, I am grateful for this experience", even when struck by a disaster or tragedy? It does not make any sense. Can you elaborate on this idea? Of course, to an ordinary mind, mixed in chaos and confusion it does not make any sense. As a matter of fact, the following should be recited many times as a mantra-the sacred word.

I AM GRATEFUL!

The moment you utter this affirmation sincerely, you are out of the doldrum of despair and desperation. Understand gratitude as a mind cleanser. It is the elixir for removing negativity. Let us take an example (real life), and see how this technique will bring an everlasting and harmonious solution.

Let us say that Patricia, received a Divorce notice in the mail from her husband. She knew that her husband had 'something' going on with another woman. But she did not think, that he will seek a divorce. "She thinks that she is not ready for this". With two small children to take care of and herself not working, she thinks that her world came down crashing on her.

As soon as she got the letter, she followed to the letter, the recitation of this mantra-

"I am grateful for the experience".

The very act of reciting this 'mantra' removes her from a defensive position. She is not reacting to this, as the most of the people in similar situation will do. Instead, she is acting. When you act you are a master, and when you react you are a slave. Patricia chose to be the master of the circumstances, rather than a victim. That very state of mind puts her in the driver's seat.

The negative reaction, which is usually the case in similar circumstances, is diffused by being grateful. The mind devoid of any negativity is ready to tackle any problem at hand. She will continue to be grateful, and wishes her husband well, not ill, in his new relationship. Knowing fully well that you cannot force somebody to love you, and also knowing fully well that whatever happens is for the better. She goes on with her life, engaging an attorney to handle the legal matters, and instructing him that she is not interested in having a contentious battle. She wishes her children's father, to handle the situation amicably.

Apart from all the financial matters, because she remains grateful for what happened her state of mind is one of harmony. She does not go through an emotional turmoil which eventually will affect the health and well-being. Many women in similar circumstances, will fall victim to life threatening diseases. Instead, she decided to keep her family, and be there, 'full time' for her little children, who are too young to understand what is going on.

Gratitude, simply cleanses your mind. It takes you to the Higher power, or God whatever name you choose to call IT for every solution. A mind devoid of negativity is 'divine', divinity alone dwells there. And a ' divinely absorbed mind', is a creative mind, as it can attract anything from anywhere to find solution to your pressing problem, however challenging it may appear to be at the outset.

This is the healing power of gratitude. It simply produces harmony instead of discord. It is not what happens to you that matters, but how you perceive it, or process the information. Gratitude is an invitation to Divine Intervention, not dictating what should happen, but surrendering to the Higher Power to be in charge of the situation. You abstain, from wishing ill to anyone, but deliberately 'wishing well', to all parties involved. You wish for others what you wish for yourself (Jainism). The same is echoed in Bible and the Golden rule, that you treat people the way you like to be treated. A grateful mind is the abode of abundance. It can attrct, wealth, health, harmony, happiness, why even salvation or freedom from bondage. The key is training your mind to be a grateful mind. Always remind yourself that,

'GRATITUDE MUST BE THE ONLY ATITUDE IN LIFE'

Question 9

What is negativity? How does it affect our daily life?

The best way to define negativity is to compare it with darkness, the absence of light. Wherever there is no harmony there is negativity. The Law of Harmony is the Supreme Law of the Spirit. The very unity of spirit, that state of tranquility, is harmony. Where there is harmony, there is peace and plenty where there is no harmony there is negativity. Negativity can be compared to darkness. Darkness is the condition caused by the absence of light. Similarly, the moment harmony is introduced, negativity disappears.

Gratitude is the eternal light, that erases the darkness of negativity. It can be compared to the Sun who is the ultimate dispeller of darkness in the Universe. Just like light and darkness cannot coexist, gratitude and negativity cannot coexist. Thus, a heart filled with gratitude cannot entertain, any kind of negativity. Thus, people who remain grateful at all the times, cannot be the victims of negativity, because they are immersed in gratitude at all times, and they cannot see anything but positive. Because of the subtle operation of the Law of Belief, they remain grateful. Their every moment is a hymn to this attitude.

Question 10

How does Negativity affect your life?

Negativity has multiple faces. Vanity is a face negativity. Anger, fear, hate, depression and even despair is made of negativity. Come to think of it. Negativity is the mother of all ailments both bodily, mental and emotional. It is the raw material with which all negative emotions are created. It drains one's positive energy and makes him vulnerable and exposed to all kinds of diseases. The immune system breakdowns, due to the constant exposure to negative energy what poison does to the human body, negative energy does to the human mind.

Question 11

What is the common negative energy exposure?

Gossip - (you are sipping the negativity that arises during the gossip exercise) and worse, we do not even know about it.

Remedy: talk well of others.

Hate - A very dangerous exposure to negative energy. It unleashes negativity into the system, it profusely drains our positivity.

Remedy - Love what you hate. Bless that hates you.

Fear - Fear is a very common and yet little understood negative emotion. It has very different stages, starting with simple fear, if left unchecked, it can lead to panic, and anxiety attacks.

Remedy - Do not allow fear to take root in your mind. Develop a 'FAITH", a faith in higher power-God. Recite loudly, "when God is with me, who could be against me".

When fearful thoughts emerge, recite with emotion-

'I am grateful for this Thought Experience'.

The outstanding virtue of gratitude is that

'IT NEUTRALISES NEGETIVITY AND NO

PRODUCTION OF FEAR IS POSSIBLE.

To make the impact of Negative emotions graphic, let me tell you a story of Devil and his weapons. Once Devil put on display all the 'wares' (weapons) he uses to enter the mind of man. The display looks like one below:

HATE=SWORD

FEAR=KNIFE

VANITY=HAMMER

JEALOUSY=WEDGE

DESPAIR=SYRINGE

One of the visitors to the display (exhibition) asked the Devil, of all the items displayed, a simple looking Syringe called Despair is the most expensive. Why is it so? The Devil replied, that the Syringe is simple looking, but you do not know that it is deadly in its results. When all my weapons like Hate, Fear, jealousy and Vanity fail, I inject a dose of despair in the mind of man and slowly but surely it will spread throughout his system, and the rest is history. Thus, it is clear that a 'Dose of Despair' is all that takes the devil to bring down even the brightest mind among men.

MIND BODY CONNECTION

We all know that mind and body are connected. Now the modern medical science after so many years of research has announced that there is something called Mind. It can cause disease and ailments. The very term 'psychosomatic'-means psyche affecting soma-the body.

Every emotion is the manifestation of the Mind Body connection. A positive emotion like Love, Compassion, Mercy, Forgiveness, Care all impact positively the soma, while negative emotions like Fear, Jealousy, Hate, Vanity, Anger etc. affect the 'soma' negatively.

In Molecules of Emotion, Dr. Candice Pert explains the biological impact of various emotions based on extensive research she has done in this emerging field of science. Even when Scientific research was not even conceived, the Great Mental Scientist declared:

"YE FIRST SEEK THE KINGDOM OF GOD (DOMAIN OF SPIRIT) and its righteousness, everything shall be added unto you".

The Supreme Law of Spirit is harmony. Once you learn to dwell on the plane of harmony, you remain healed at all the times. Healing means that feeling of oneness where there is no conflict, where there is no stress. You are literally living in the present. Living in the present means that you are at peace with yourself and the universe. Gratitude, being the mother of all positive healing emotions, helps you focus on the present without being dragged into the painful past or being in anxiety about the future. Leave the painful past to the life's mourners and the dancing fancy of the future to the dreamers. They both equally miss the present. Healing is possible only in the present.

Question 12

How does Gratitude, help you live in the present moment, and let go of the past and the future?

Gratitude is the only attitude that accepts 'What is'. It does simply say, I am grateful for this experience". It does not alter the experience and comment that it should have been the other way. You have heard the expression, 'man, wants things hot when it is cold, and wants it cold when it is hot. It only shows he is never satisfied. Always trying to fantasize what is not. It's an act of escapism, it is running away from the present moment.

Let us take a concrete example. A man, let us call him Patrick, who was summoned to his boss's office. The boss said "Patrick, I am sorry, due to corporate policy of downsizing operation in the US we have to let you go". Patrick's head started spinning, and he suddenly started to replay the record "in his head of the lost job two years ago. His mind started recalling the painful experience of the past when the family had to survive on one paycheck for almost a year, before he got this job. In secrecy, he was watching that mental movie of pain and suffering and guilty feeling whenever he could. Hence the Biblical expression "what I have feared has fallen upon me".

Instead of slipping back into the past, Patrick can adopt a grateful attitude to the situation. He can tell the boss in all sincerity-"Sir, you've to do what you have to do. I have no hard feeling. I am grateful for this Experience". The moment he declares his sincere heart felt gratitude for this Experience, he accepts the present he embraces it and chose to remain grateful. A mind filled with gratitude, attracts similar vibrations from the outer universe as like attracts the like. An old friend from the past could see him on the way home and mentioned to Patrick that his company has an opening for similar position or even a better position and Patrick could apply for it. It is also possible that his old boss was always impressed with Patrick's attitude and calm and level headed approach to co-workers, that when an opening came in another department, he called Patrick to apply for the job. He was hired, with his old boss's recommendations. It is said that when one door closes, seven doors open. But mostly people look at the closed door and, they miss the seven doors opening behind them.

Past is a trap, and so is the future. Do not be a 'waiter' in life. A waiter is one

who almost says "l will be okay and I can take my dream vacation, after I pay off the mortgage in three years" Do not play the waiting game? It robes of your precious present. You only live in the present and you can have everything every enjoyment in the present if you know how to enjoy. If you are watching a movie with your wife or husband, enjoy it without worrying or thinking about the 'big meeting' you have at the office on Monday. When you are at the big meeting, your mind may be wandering after a romantic scene in the movie that you watched with your wife on Sunday. You could have very well enjoyed the romantic scene in the movie with your wife on Sunday rather than thinking about the 'big meeting' on Monday.

Being grateful, helps you remain in the present. It is a facilitator who helps you enjoy the present, whatever it may be. If you are changing the diaper of your baby, enjoy it. Look into the eyes of the innocent infant and see the sparkle. Remain in the moment, careful not to hurt the infant in anyway. Give the infant the feeling that at this moment there are only two people in the world-just you and the baby. Remain fully absorbed in the moment, with whatever task at hand. Observe your mind, and make sure that your thoughts remain focused in the present moment, and the mind does not slip back into the past or surge forward into the future. If it does, bring it back to the present moment.

Just be in the present and enjoy whatever you are doing.

Gratitude is a mind stabilizer. It stabilizes the mind to remain in the present. It helps to prevent the mind from slipping back into the past or surging forward into the uncertain future. Both are equally bad, as each one causes you to miss the precious present, being grateful releases you from the task of defending you, from whatever situation you are.

Question 13

What is the role of gratitude in healing?

The healing power of gratitude is very evident from the state of mind created when a person is grateful. A grateful mind is a fearless mind. It accepts things as they are, without any preconceived idea that things ought to be in this way like the modern saying, "it is my way or the highway". When you accept things as they are, when you, live in the present, without fear, the infinite healing presence which is everywhere, awakens in your body and mind. There is no resistance from your mind to the healing power to do its work. Healing means to make whole and where there is conflict, where there is resistance, 'whole' cannot be present. And the healing power of gratitude neutralizes the fear; it harmonizes the mind and body, and the divine healing power flows in. As the old saying goes, "the doctor dresses the wound and God heals it!

Of all the negative emotions we combat, fear a is one of the very deadly ones. Fear of disease and fear of subsequent death send the people to a bottomless pit of misery and suffering. They keep watching the mental movies of the suffering and the pain, and literally invite those conditions in their life. Again, as we mentioned above, 'What I have feared has fallen upon me'. By thinking negatively, you literally create, that which you have feared.

The ancient UPANISHADS written more than five thousand years ago declares that God is the eternal now. The higher power is not in the past or in the future. It exists Now and Here. You cannot enjoy the bliss of your being, if you are not in the present. All the Luminaries of the world who preceded us, got inspired in the present to write divinely ordained scriptures like Bible, Koran, Bhagavad Gita or Talmud. Inspiration is instant in the present moment not tomorrow or next week.

An exercise to Experience the Present Moment

Write down ten thoughts as they flash in your mind:

Awareness arises

Wait for a thought

The thought comes

Continue writing

A familiar song

Childhood

Mother

Mother's wisdom

The day she died

Healing takes place in the present moment. Gratitude enables us to focus in the present. Even when the mind is running after the painful past or future, being grateful enables one to bring it back to the present moment. Gratitude is an anchor for present, it produces awareness instantly. The stillness of mind, the awareness of the present is absolutely essential for healing to take place. Gratitude indeed is a facilitator. A few flashing moments of stillness where there is a void, when the mind is absent, What Zen masters called the Satori one can experience with gratitude. Because gratitude neutralizes, negativity the mind is fresh and unattached to any thought. It is a cleansing moment for the mind where there is no thought to attend to, the stillness alone is felt.

As the Old Testament says, 'Be still' and know that I am god'. In the great hall of stillness where like a magnificent night immersed in sprawling moonlight inducing mother nature to be meditative, one can know the presence of God. When you experience the present moment, the gap between two thoughts widens and in that gap of stillness mind does not exist.

Question 14

Is it correct to say that, gratitude permits rather produces 'an acceptance' of 'what is, instead of 'what should be'?

Indeed, grateful attitude expresses gratitude for whatever comes on our way. It simply accepts it, embraces it and still remains in a reverential mood. The greatest agent of change is alchemy. The main problem we all face in our life is our inability to change. As long as we do not change, we invite to our life 'the same old' experience. This mother of all healing emotions paves the way for a change to a radical transformation from suffering to understanding, from understanding to acceptance and total surrender. In that attitude of surrender all resistances break down. There is no more feeling that "it should be". Instead, you are willing and able and happy to accept 'what is'. This is the moment of transformation. You are ready to leap into the world of better experience. Total surrender is not a sign of weakness. It is the sign of inner understanding. It recognizes our true nature which is Divine, It recognizes our heritage which is nothing but inexhaustible power-the power to stimulate, the power to inspire and the power to create. Before transformation, we were in a state of rebellion, we do not like what we see and kept on complaining which solidified the same old experience. In the transformed stage, we accept whatever comes; express our gratitude, for it knowing fully well that it's transient nature. This too shall come to pass. Nothing is permanent except the in dweller that emotive power pulsating in us, which can transform the unmanifested into any form we want. You have to only provide that prototype or the mold for the unmanifested spirit to pour into it.

The prototype is created when we create a burning desire, and it is only a matter of time that the physical manifestation takes place. That creative activity where the unmanifested becomes the manifested, is possible in the present moment. Thus, Gratitude is the Great TRANSFORMER-it helps us to focus on the present by accepting what is instead of wallowing in the past, and going through the mental movies of pain, suffering and ensuing frustration. It is projecting the same old, like the frog got trapped in a well, where it is a prisoner, unless it can jump out of the well to its freedom.

The moment you choose to remain in the present you are ready for the freedom - freedom from the same old, freedom from frustration, freedom from the prison from your own negativity and complete freedom from being a victim to a victor. You discover your own creative process and inherit power to create whatever you want to create out of the unmanifested. It is not only possible to create your world, but it empowers you to build your own fortress of power, peace and tranquility. Gratitude takes place to center point of your own true nature-the kingdom of God-that domain of Harmony where there is only blessing-a feeling of peace and more gratitude. Hence it is said in the Bible 'Ye First seek the kingdom of god and its righteousness, everything shall be added unto you'. Thus, a heart filled with gratitude is ready to receive more blessings.

Being a Transforming Agent Gratitude helps us to open our eyes to the vast vistas of possibilities, it helps us to breakdown the true barriers that exist between the painful past and resourceful present. It is present alone which is pregnant with possibilities. Not the past nor the future, as both are imaginary and only create a prison for our mind to roam around in a circle, without reaching anywhere, or reaching the same place we started.

The same pain, Frustration, and suffering.

The great Buddha said, "Pain is inevitable, but suffering is optional". It is easy to face pain, but very difficult to face suffering. Suffering takes place in the realm of mind. It is imagination running around like a mad elephant in the field of time. It can be only checked being in the PRESENT.

Suffering is in the field of time. Time assumes space. There can be no time without space. Time by definition is a period taken by a body to move from point A to point B. If there is no time, there is no space. One shadows the other. Gratitude thus enables us to transcend both Time and Space.

Being in the present also means that you are in the field of possibilities and not limitations. Limitations are placed by our being in the past. The limitations of the past experienced by us as rebuke, insult, injury and defeat and failures are played and replayed in our memory record, that you will ultimately become the epicenter of limitations'.

Gratitude, thus jump-start your own transformation, it creates a passage - a passage from serfdom to freedom, limitations to possibilities, from past pain and suffering to peace and harmony. You have learnt to say 'goodbye' to blame game. You have no one to blame, as you understand the Spiritual Side of You. You come to the conclusion that you are not this body, nor this mind but the indweller the driver and not the car. Hence

Jesus asserted 'I am He' - 'Me and My father are one'.

Question 15

How can we apply the principle of gratitude to solve everyday problems? For example, I am not happy with the way I look.

I am overweight and feel bad about it. Can gratitude help me shed my weight?

Of course, without any doubt. The weight you have put on did not happen overweight. That is total effects of so many years of accumulated negative thoughts. Somewhere I read, 'your history writes your biology': rather than dwelling in the past for those painful memories, we focus on the present for our mantra-

I AM GRATEFUL FOR THIS EXPERIENCE

Unconsciously, we seek solution for our problems, such as hurt injury, pain, betrayal and a lot of other negative emotions in the least desired and detrimental solution like alcohol, food or even dangerous drugs. Food addiction is a common problem among many men and women in the present time. Lack of self-esteem, though it appears in many disguises, also adds to ones craving for food. I call it unconscious eating. Once you become conscious of what you eat and why you eat there will be radical changes in the food habits. Along with changes in food habit and elevated self-esteem, you will eat healthy food moderately and follow a food regiment of exercises both for the body and mind. Your body is the shadow of your mind. A clean mind produces a healthy (a clean) body. Working on your body without working on your daily thoughts, is an exercise in futility.

Always ask this question. Where does my body exist? Only in your mind is the answer. A mind which has become the dwelling place of negativity and disharmonious thoughts like hate, anger, jealousy and lack of self-esteem, needs to be elevated by constant regimentation before you can see changes taking place in your body. The body will definitely follow your mind, as it is the effect of the sum total of your thoughts.

CHAPTER X

Thoughts and Habits

Thoughts and habits are both friends and enemies at the same time. The art of thinking is a mental exercise as it consumes lot of mental energy depending upon the intensity and volume of thoughts. The more you think on a subject intensely, the more tense and tired you become. We all experience the tension and stress when we are studying for the finals or a highly competitive professional examination. Our brain is engaged in the intellectual exercise consuming lot of oxygen. Many people do not like to think and they expect others to think for them. Thus, they can conserve the energy and avoid the tension and stress involved in doing so. Habits on the contrary are automatic, and involve minimum thinking. Here they are the friends of thinking as they conserve the mental energy which can be employed for other more useful purposes.

Let us imagine that you have to think about driving to work in every detail. You have to think about starting the engine, changing the gear, turning the lights on and putting the gear in "reverse". Think of the days you were learning driving twenty years ago. If you have to think about every aspect of driving today, you will not be in the office before lunch time. Most likely it will be an agonizing experience. Two decades of driving made it a habit and you are an expert driver allowing the mind to wander during the driving. You can cruise at eighty or ninety miles not thinking about it until the driver in front of you applies sudden break, and you do the same thing automatically out of habit to avoid a crash. Thus, the habit of driving saves you lot of time, energy, mental energy expended and the stress of learning driving every day. Thus, the habit of driving has become a friend of thought, as you need not think about it. Habit can also be an enemy at times. For example, you get up every day at 5.00AM to go to work as you have to report by 7.00AM. On Saturday you do not go to work and you like to sleep an hour more. In all probability you will wake up at 5.00AM out of habit as the body is used to getting up at that time. Even if you did not set the alarm, body's own clock makes you get up at 5.00AM. You cannot resist the temptation to get up at 5.00AM.

Habit is a merciless master. We need to cultivate the habits that add to our quality of life, and break the habits that are detrimental to our emotional and physical well-being. Life is after all, a parade of thoughtless habits, and we need to consciously analyze the present habits to improve our life and self-transformation.

HABIT EDITING

Habit editing is an art. Every habit is the sum total of repeated rituals. Either knowingly or unknowingly you repeat certain rituals and over a period of time they become permanent companions following you like a shadow. Most of the habits are formed unconsciously over a period of time. Some of them are beneficial and most of them are not beneficial, like chewing your nail, unconscious eating, including eating to please.

Need for Habit Editing:

Unless you edit your habits, you will not be conscious of the impact of the habits that have become a part of you. Habit Editing also helps you to identify the beneficial habits or harmful habits. Beneficial habit you need to retain and encourage them by fortifying. When you shift your attention, you convert unconscious habits to conscious habits formation.

My first habit challenge!

More than a decade ago, I had the habit of chewing my nail. I used to do it in my childhood as I was a bit shy and a timid child. Even after becoming an adult, it followed me everywhere. May be as an adult, I stopped chewing my nails in public, though in the privacy of loneliness, I still relished the secret habit. Many times, I was embarrassed to show my nails in public. I was also not good in trimming my nails neat and clean. I was also too embarrassed to go to a saloon alone as I thought it was only for girls and men do not go there to cut the nails. My wife always asked me “what do you do with your nails”? I simply kept quiet and I was even more embarrassed. But in 2012 at the age of sixty-eight I was diagnosed with type two diabetes as “late onset of diabetes” by my primary care physician. He also advised against cuts and bruises on my hands and feet as they will take more time to heal. This is the time I decided to go to a nail saloon, and when the place was less crowded, I showed up embarrassingly as I thought I was invading a female only saloon. One thing is true even today after a decade that more than 90% of the patrons at the nail saloon are women. I confessed to my nail expert that I am in the habit of chewing my nail and that is why they are uneven and bleeding. She was very supportive and made me more comfortable in my bones. She did a good job and she did both pedicure and manicure, and she said I had good nails except that my feet had some kind of fungi, for which she recommended a kind of cream. After I started going to the nail saloon, I stopped nail biting, and my nails become healthy and professionally groomed. They looked very good and appealing as a reward! When I was in the ER one time, the ER nurse even commended "Gopi, you have very good nails" and they do not need any ER treatment. I felt proud of my manicurist whom I visit at least once in six weeks. The habit of nail biting disappeared, as my nail looks always shiny and clean and many of my young female associates comment on them very frequently, although it comes with a cost of $75.00 per trip to the Saloon. But I am not embarrassed any more about my nails. Needless to say, my wife was very happy of my welcome change that was an added encouragement. My children noticed the clean nail too!

Our Three Tools of Engagement:

We human beings, no matter who we are and what we do for a living, have three tools of engagement with the universe. They are our thoughts, our speech and our action also known as TSA (Thought, Speech and Action). The integrity of our habit is based on TSA alignment. Many times, thought, speech and action do not align and our habits are not permanent as they can wear off due to inadequate repetition. Our habits are formed not based on the lapse of time, but based on the number of repetitions over a period of time. That is why consistent practice of a certain ritual is more important to the formation of a certain behaviors. This consistency of practice separates a professional athlete or a musician from an amateur athlete or a musician. They repeat their rituals consistently over a period of time and most of the time during the entire life. It is practice, practice and more practice in the art of the game that you want to master regardless of basketball, golf or vocal or instrumental music.

Inventory of Habits

Before you edit your habits, make an inventory of habits you want to edit. The area of behaviors you want to improve, and if you are willing to invest your time and money in changing your thoughts, speech and action you can master any behaviors you choose. Now the neuro scientists have come to the conclusion that you can rewire your brain, by repeating the same tasks again and again. Our ancestors without the help of FMRI (it was not invented) knew repetition is the mother of perfection. In other words, "the neurons that fire together, wire together", creating a formidable force. This also emphasizes the need to consistent repetition of the rituals that alter the position of the neurons in the brain.

An example of Habit Inventory

Current Habits	Desired Habits
Easily discouraged	Resilience (Cultivate)
React to people, events and conditions	Respond to people events and conditions
Procrastinate in taking actions	Swift Action
Getting Angry	Practice forgiveness
Getting Afraid	Start worshipping the fear (becoming empowered)
Easily insulted	Feel the self-worth
Too Egoistic	Be Humble

Feeling Depressed	Be Grateful
Being absent minded	Cultivate awareness
I am selfish	Practice Charity
Being Mortal	Ask the question "who dies"?
Problem of Clutter	One minute cleaning

Take one habit at a time:

We may want to change many habits in our life. The best way to tackle the habit formation is to take one habit at a time and work on it for the next ninety days. Select the most important habit you want to change, and acquire mastery over one habit will also boost your confidence in your ability. Awareness is the foundation of the new habit formation. Just like a builder builds a house brick by brick, you can change your habit thought by thought, speech by speech and action by action. Awareness is the common thread that weave the tapestry of a habit no matter what habit you want to alter.

My Second Habit Challenge:

I embarked on a radical objective of becoming a writer and a published author from a reader, and I resorted to a method of public declaration to affect this habit change. I read somewhere that a radical method of changing identity is to announce in public and now you find yourself in a bind, to change your identity as you already made commitment in public, and you cannot back out of your commitment. I thought I was really crazy to undertake such a commitment in spite of my weakness and lack of resources. It was in 1995 December during the holiday season I announced my desire to publish a book under the title 'Mental Science 101'.

My second son Hari used to be a voracious reader in high school and our common hang out place was Borders Book Store in Oakbrook, Illinois. This time of the year many authors used to come there for book signing. One evening when we were at the Borders Book Store, there was a book signing going on, and I and Hari listened to an author speak, and bought a copy of the book. After we bought a copy of the Book, I told Hari who was in second year of High School, "Hey Hari your dad wants to publish Mental Science 101, in less than two years and would like to have a book signing here at Borders". Hari was always supportive of me like all my children and he said "why not. you can do it Ach (father)". Encouraged by his words, and to display my ultimate craziness I approached Pat, the lady who arranged the book signing for the authors. She was very supportive too and calmly said "Mr. Nair, you tell me when you want to come here for the book signing". She also added, "you and your son are good customers of Borders and I will have no problem convincing my boss". I was not sure if she took me seriously or she thought I was joking.

After I made the public announcement, I was in a panic mode, and doubts began to creep into my consciousness. First of all, I have never thought about publishing a book and secondly, I learned English as a Second Language as I migrated from India more than three decades ago. I seriously thought I put my foot in my mouth, and could be an embarrassment to my own high school aged son. Of course, I have been a student of Mental Science since the eighties reading the books of luminaries like Judge Thomas Troward, William James the famous Harvard Psychologist and Dr. Joseph Murphy, the author of the Power of your subconscious mind. It was a frantic leap for me to convert myself from an ardent reader to a professional writer. I always believed in the power of the universe to make your dream come true and I started reading those books from a writer's point of view. I also started writing a few pages on a daily basis, first thing in the morning before getting off to work.

Now I did one crazier thing, as I started to tell my boss at MetLife, and many of my clients and friends that I am writing a book on Mental Science 101. My boss who also hailed from Kerala, India had a Master's Degree in Business from North-Western University of Chicago. He was also very supportive of my writing rather my wild adventure. To make the long story short, I had a first copy of my book Mental Science 101, by summer of 1997. I went back to Pat from Borders Book Store with the book and she could not believe her eyes as I showed her a copy of my Book. But she kept her word, and arranged a book signing for me, and many more book signing in almost all the stores in Chicago land and Northwest Indiana. Since the book was self-published by me, I was able to sell more than a thousand copies and it was good enough for an amateur author who literally and figuratively trespassed into the publishing world, by really putting his foot in the mouth.

Now after almost three decades I self-published more than ten books like Gopis Gratitude journal, One hundred essays on Gratitude, and Tablets of Emotional wisdom. Now I am convinced the truth behind the old Chinese saying that 'a journey of a thousand miles begins with a single step' to translate it into the writer's parlance, I may say that a writing journey begins with writing one paragraph and repeating over and over during one's life time. I personally think that if I can publish more than ten books, anybody can write and publish any number of books even though the path of an author is never paved with golden bricks, and for that matter with any bricks.

Needless to say, that my son Hari along with his two brothers Sai and Sabari are all my core cheer leaders. I am indeed honored and humbled by their invaluable support and cheer leading. There are many other habits I need to change to transform my entire life. The famous author of Atomic Habits is my habit guru namely James Clear who has done extensive research in the art of habit change and personal transformation. As James Clear emphatically pointed out in his book Atomic Habits, "I fulfilled my potential. And I believe the concepts in this book can help you fulfill your potential too". After all' life is nothing but a parade of habits acquired knowingly or unknowingly. Habits editing is the art of looking at your habits consciously and undo the habits that harm you, and cultivate the habit that benefit you in the long run. The small rituals you practice every day will have the magical effect of transforming you over a period. The miracle of compounding effect, with marginal gains every time your perform the rituals, is mind blowing and in the financial world it is known as the magic of compound interest.

Over a period of twenty-five years, I have been able to articulate my writing habit that resulted in writing eleven books, and over three hundred articles and linked in posts. It is not to display my arrogant boasting but to share my experience and power of taming habits to change you own outlook and personality. You ultimately become the carrier of your own habit as they become an integral part of who you are!

The Story of the Mailman:

More than half a century ago, while I was growing up in a small village in the South Indian state of Kerala, I was very often intrigued by my mother's extraordinary behavior. Since my older brother was away working in Northern India, we used to get mail regularly from him at least once every month. I still remember the mailman whose name was Kesavan Nair, a heavyset middle-aged man with swollen feet, who used to announce his arrival before he entered the fenced compound. My mother was always very pleased with him, and my older sister and I would gather around her to witness the "event" of my mother receiving the mail and the money order. After signing the money order and receiving the letter, my mother would offer the mailman lunch, which was always a custom in our home. After the simple lunch, my mother would give him a gratuity of one rupee, I, being the youngest child, always had certain privileges, and using that, questioned my mother about giving the gratuity to the mailman every time he delivers the mail. My mother said, "Gopi, you have to be grateful to the mailman because he brings good news from your brother. A small gratuity was only a token of gratitude to the mailman." Even though it satisfied my curious mind, I still did not "get it". But one thing I remember about that mailman until he retired, or any mailman for that matter, never brought any bad news to my mother.

Thus, I learned the virtue of gratitude from my own mother at the age of twelve. The noble experience with the mailman stayed with me throughout my adult life. When I was working as an Insurance Salesman and all throughout my sales career spanning over five decades, and even today I am very grateful to my clients. I sincerely remind me every day that it is my group of all clients who enable me to put dinner on my family's dinner table. I remain eternally indebted to thousands of my friends and clients who helped me become successful in the art of selling. There were years in my sales career, I really did not know where the next meal was coming from. But my attitude of gratitude helped me remain positive and the grateful mental attitude always redirected my attention to the many things I had to be grateful for. My wife Lalitha understood the nature of my career and was always there to support me and she never had any complaints during the half a century I have known her. My children are always my cheerleaders, when I was facing periodic sales competition. They all accompanied me during my sales conferences like Leaders Conference and Presidents Conference while working with MetLife.

I have been practicing gratitude as a way of life since 2016, and in addition to my expression of gratitude to all my clients and well-wishers I started looking at life and its challenges through the prism of gratitude. Even after twenty-eight years since my mother left her mortal frame, her voice is still ringing in my ears "Gopi whatever God gives you (whatever challenges you face in life) receive them with both hands (fully accept them) and say thank you, it could have been worse". Even today at the age of eighty, I have never come across with a practical problem-solving technique, as I received from my mother. She was my Wharton School of Business, though she herself had only completed fifth grade in formal schooling. I was very fortunate to drink at her well of wisdom. She was my spiritual mentor and the greatest cheer leader I have come across in my life. Since God could not come himself/herself to hold my hand in time of need, my mother was deputed to fill in the void. She did in fact fill in the void as well as the Almighty will do under similar circumstances.

Developing Rituals of Practicing Gratitude"

When I started the habit of practicing gratitude, I developed a number of daily rituals that constitute my everyday practice. It is the consistent practice of rituals on a daily basis that results in formation of a certain habits. These daily rituals are the foundation of a process that makes you a person that you want to become. My goal was to become a grateful person, and more importantly be a gratitude practitioner, one who can face all the challenges that life throws at you with an attitude of gratitude. I wanted to rewire my brain with an attitude of gratitude as I learned from the neuro scientists that neurons "that fire together wire together", strengthening the neuronal pathways. I designed a few rituals for daily practice that can fortify my behaviors of practicing gratitude as a way of life. The elements of my gratitude rituals are as follow:

One minute gratitude practice

Upon rising in the morning.

As soon as I wake up in the morning before getting out of bed, I recite three times:

I am grateful to the Universe

I am grateful to the Universe I am grateful to the Universe

Breakfast with Gratitude:

The second ritual in the practice of gratitude is breakfast with gratitude. Almost all of us follow certain rituals (simple task) before we get ready for the day. You can use the time to express your gratitude by writing in a Gratitude Journal, you can express your gratitude to five people to whom you are grateful, for their contribution to your life. You can start with your parents, siblings, grandparents and other members of the extended family. You can also include your teachers, mentors and the others who went out of their way to help you become who you are today. You can also express five events in your life that stand out in your memory like the day you graduated from high school, college or graduate school. The day you met your sweet heart in high school, or the day you got married, or the day your first child was born. As you keep on writing you will runout of past people and past events and this is the time you can choose people and events from your everyday life. Rather than becoming mechanical, let these words and expressions sprout from the bottom of your heart as you pour your emotions into the writing.

Gopi's Gratitude Journal:

In 2016 after I decided to practice gratitude, I was looking for a Gratitude Journal in Barnes and Noble, the famous Book Store in our town. I was not really impressed with any of the journals, I found in the book store as they were bland or just a notebook printed as a Gratitude Journal. Since I could not find a journal I liked, I decided to write "Gopi's Gratitude Journal" which provides a daily journal to enhance the benefits of daily practice.

Maintaining a Gratitude Journal is an integral part of practicing gratitude as it weaves an attitude of Gratitude in dealing with all challenges in life. Our habits are nothing but an army of traits that protects us on daily basis in our struggle with life. Cessation of struggle is death and managing struggle is life. Managing struggle regardless whether they are related to personal relationship, financial relationship or health challenges is really a 'big deal' as it makes or breaks our life. Our ability to handle the challenges in our day-to-day affairs defines who we are, successful or not, happy or unhappy, productive or unproductive and even humane or inhumane in dealing with others. There is a great saying in Zen Buddhism "before nirvana, chopping the Woods and carrying the water, after nirvana chopping the woods and carrying the water". In that case the question arises what nirvana changes? The answer is one's own attitude. Even though the tasks are identical before and after 'nirvana' the attitude towards the tasks radically changes after 'nirvana' which is nothing but one of equanimity towards all people and all tasks, as the Zen Master has overcome likes and dislikes, 'mine and his', as the entire universe to such an enlightened person looks simply like a 'play of consciousness'. While the world around him or her is fleeting with transformative changes, the awareness alone remains 'constant', the changeless and the eternal.

The practice of gratitude and writing journal entries in one's Gratitude Journal, help the practitioner to remain in the present forgetting the past which is nothing but recycling one's own foregone emotions. Immersed in the joy of the present moment he is also free from the anxiety of tomorrow, as it is a tapestry of one's own imagination unfolding before one's mental eyes. The very transient nature of one's own life becomes apparent to the Gratitude Practitioner as she no more mourns the death of the past, nor celebrate the birth of tomorrow which again is nothing but an exercise in one's own imagination. Armed with this new insight about the very nature of our life she likes to immerse in the task at hand, giving it her undivided attention like a mother to her newborn.

TSA Alignment

Another great importance step in the practice of Gratitude is TSA Alignment, to make sure that your thoughts, speech and action are in alignment with each other every time you engage with the universe. You think, you speak, and you act, the three cardinal tools of engagement with the universe. Your thoughts must align with your speech, the words you utter and the deeds that you perform. Unless the three are aligned like stars in the sky, you are creating conflicts within yourself, and it is only a matter of time before the inner conflicts get exposed as outer conflicts that affect your very peace of mind. These inner conflicts can spill into your relationship with your spouse, your children, your siblings or even at work with your own boss or the colleagues. The best way to resolve a conflict is not to create one to begin with. Thus, TSA Alignment reminds you of the need to keep your thoughts, speech and action in alignment with each other. TSA is the heart of communication and it reduces the inner conflicts, if not erase them altogether at a future date.

TSA - Your Habit Auditor:

TSA alignment is your Habit Auditor, who certifies that your behavior is excellent, and it is the conduit to peace and happiness in life. The epitome of effective communication is TSA Alignment, that makes sure that you are creating harmonious relationship in your everyday engagement with the Universe. Just like a financial auditor pinpoints the defects of the financial status of an organization, TSA alignment reminds you of disparities in alignment between your Thoughts and Speech and the action that follows. TSA alignment is a daily reminder to correct the course of communication, to reach the maximum benefits that spin out of harmony and amity. TSA causes a steady ride through the road of life which may not be always paved with gold.

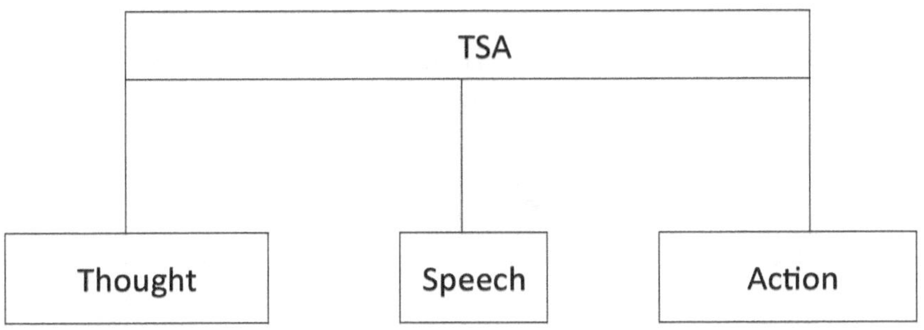

Thought Harvesting:

Thoughts come and go as in a flash. Many times, we cannot even recall the thoughts we entertained throughout the day. Thought harvesting is an art of consciously planting thoughts in one's mind about a particular habit one likes to develop. To cultivate new thoughts, one has to deliberately think about the subject one wants to develop, and regularly read on the topic. For example, if you want to become a gratitude practitioner you have to read many books on the subjects, as I did in 2016 when I decided to form the daily practice of Gratitude to improve the quality of life. I started reading and re-reading many books on the subject of Gratitude like New Testament, Bhagavad-Gita, Quran and Buddhist Text books. I discovered in the New Testament the word 'chariti' the Greek word for Gratitude is used in 157 times. Even great apostle St. Paul declared "be thankful under all circumstances". All the religious traditions extol the virtue of gratitude as a way of living not as a simple virtue. Buddhism talks about the debt of gratitude to one's parents, teachers and elders who help us shape our life in our formative years. Lord

Krishna tells Arjuna in Gita to cling to one's own duty when challenged by external influences that impede our ability to act under trying circumstances, as Arjuna focused on the past and the future where the consequences of one's actions dwell. Krishna wanted him to focus on his duty as a Warrior Prince to summon his courage to take his bow and arrow to fight his enemies. One has to practice gratitude to anchor the mind in the present moment, where one's duty alone prevails. The pain of hurting one's teachers and cousin brother or other relatives only belonged to the past which gives us a baggage of emotions. The sum and substance of Bhagavad-Gita is to 'adhere to one's duty, whatever it may be when challenged by external influences how insignificant they appear to be. All forms of worship in any religious traditions are nothing, but expressions of gratitude to the Higher Power, no matter how that power is defined in the particular tradition.

When we daily recite a few pages from the scriptures we are understanding the meaning and purpose of life and the practice of gratitude simply help us to rewire our brain by creating new neuronal pathways. Habits are automatic behavior that do not need any conscious thinking once the neurons fire and wire together in the grey matter of our brain. Thus planting the seeds of new thoughts is nothing but planting the seeds of new habits.

Just like a farmer selects carefully the seeds that he wants to plant in the fertile soil, we all can select carefully the thoughts that we want to see harvested in the fertile soil of our mind. But in our adult life most of us cling to the old habits we all formed with the help of our parents, siblings, teachers and the society we grew up. But we all have the ability to do habit editing, and by a careful examination of habits, we can cling to the habits that are useful for our personal growth and discard those which are not conducive to our growth and prosperity. Awareness is the fuel that runs the engine of our life. In all areas of our life like thought, speech and action we need to be aware. Habit editing is one of the methods of awareness training, which is an essential component of personal transformation. As James Clear articulates in his best seller 'Atomic Habits, daily repetition of certain rituals that create new habits or strengthen the weaker ones, creates a better version of who you are, and what type of experience you come to enjoy in everyday life.

When I started to cultivate the habit of gratitude, my objective was to become a Gratitude Practitioner, embracing a new way of life, in my personal, business, social and spiritual life. When I was a child, taking in all my surroundings like a sponge, my mother always wanted me to go to our temple and offer at the Shrine, flowers, coconut or butter in addition to my prayers. I always wondered, if God created the universe, and all the wealth therein, why does He/She need my flowers coconut or butter. It did not make any sense to me even though I did not question my mother due to my respect and appreciation for her for the sacrifices she endured to raise the six of us as a single mother. Once I started reading more about gratitude and its magical impact on our lives, it dawned on me whatever we do in the name of God in all religious tradition, is nothing but a token of our own appreciation and reverence for the creator. Besides, a daily practice of gratitude can make our mind calm and collected even when emotions run high, that threaten our own sanity. Gratitude is a mind cleanser, an agent of clarity, a catalyst that can erase traces of negativity from the shores of human mind.

When I started the practice of gratitude in 2016, I noticed two important changes in my own behavior. My tendency to judge other people has radically changed for the better. Almost all of us have a tendency to criticize others, and that tendency has started receding into the background. Today I am able to empathize with others, as I am trying to step into their shoes, rather than finding fault with them for their shortfalls and inadequacies. I am more focused about my own deficiencies rather than pointing out at others. “Everybody sings his own tunes” my mother used to tell me even though the import of her wisdom many times eluded me. Everybody is programmed in certain way, was the summary of what mother meant to say and after more than half a century of pondering over her wisdom, I get it now. Our background, education, culture and upbringing have influenced our behavior in such a way that it is almost impossible to change it now, no matter how hard we try. Habit editing is the first step towards any behavioral change we can undertake to transform ourselves to a better version ourselves. Habit editing is a very effective tool of transformation if practised diligently as the daily baby steps that we take make amazing changes in the long run.

Habits change our Identity:

Even before 2016, when I wanted to become a gratitude practitioner, I was grateful to my clients, my parents, my wife and children as they all reminded me of the sacrifices they made to make my journey enjoyable and smooth through the terrains of earth. My expressions of gratitude always spring from the bottom of my heart, rather than from the shallow surface of my lips. Once I started editing and correcting my gratitude behaviour, my very outlook towards life in general and people in particular, gradually began to change for the better. The daily rituals of gratitude prayer, breakfast with gratitude, TSA alignment, and the frequent use of gratitude 'mantra' help me become a Gratitude Practitioner always trying to see the Universe, through the prism of a grateful attitude.

I am grateful for the experience:

"I am grateful for the experience", has become my mantra, even when I am confronted by life's challenges. Whenever you are confronted by life challenges, most of the time unexpectedly, greet that experience by reciting three times "I am grateful for the experience", "I am grateful for the experience", "I am grateful for the experience".

Recite this mantra aloud as it has spiritual benefits, as the vibration of recitation rumble through your nervous system. Gratitude denotes acceptance, just the opposite of denial. It is human nature to blame others when unpleasant things happen in our life. Accepting responsibility is the first step towards solving any problem in life, no matter how hard it appears to be, when you deny the experience that is happening in your life you are trying to ignore it by denying the fact. When you are grateful for the experience you are simply accepting the fact that it has happened in your life, and you are ready to deal with it, no matter what!

I put this practice of mantra, to a real-life challenge in 2023, and the results were astounding. It was April 22, 2023 at 11.20 a.m., I was talking to a client and all of a sudden, I felt weakness on my left hand, as I was holding the telephone in that hand. In a couple of minutes, my phone fell to the floor and I knew that I am having a stroke. I decided to handle it with my gratitude 'mantra' as I recited aloud:

"I am grateful for the experience", "I am grateful for the experience", "I am grateful for the experience".

The recitation made me calm without being panic about my condition. First, I thought about calling my eldest son Sai, who lives in the same city, hardly ten minutes away from me. Then I thought about the emotional turmoil he would have to go through upon hearing the disturbing news. Empathy sets in, as I realized the situation of any human being, who has to hear his or her father who is on the other line, saying that he is having a stroke. So I decided against that. I was still alert and calm and called 911. The operator was very friendly and supportive as she remained on the line until paramedics arrived. The paramedics were professionals and they went through the check list of treating a stroke patient. With their permission, I called my son Sai, and requested him to meet me at the Elmhurst ER, where I was heading in an ambulance. Since I was calm, I could feel the same calmness in him, as he realized the best course of action under the circumstances is to go to ER in an ambulance. Since the paramedics were in charge of me, they did all the communication with the ER. We reached the ER, in less than half an hour, and the medical team with ER nurses and doctors were ready to take me in. Even the neurologist arrived in the ER very shortly to take over the treatment of a stroke patient. I was alert and calm during the ordeal, as I was mentally thinking and feeling the gratitude towards the paramedics and the entire ER Medical team. I thought, I had a mild stroke and my demeanor with the help of gratitude mantra help me to handle a very stressful situation with extra ordinary calm and alertness. Needless to say, I was very grateful to my gratitude mantra, for giving the courage to face a life-threatening challenge without being panic stricken. In a few minutes, my son came to the ER and he was relieved to see me smiling as usual. This is my first test of putting gratitude mantra to work in real life situation. It was amazing, and the calmness I felt during the ordeal blew my mind off.

The second change I noticed in 2016 after I have started practicing gratitude, is my tendency to blame others started to fade away almost completely. It was not in my nature to blame others for my handicaps, and still there were occasions when I felt a kind of negativity to others when they did not perform their best. After I have started practicing gratitude, I have developed awareness not to blame others even in my thought, which is invisible. Blaming others is a sheer waste of time and energy as we do not have a clear picture of the circumstances in which the other person acted. Every time we blame another individual for our own inadequacies or short comings, there is also an element of judgment about the behavior of the other person. I remind as a part of my gratitude practice to take full responsibility for my thought, speech and action, the three tools of engagement with the Universe. Like any other harmful habits, we can learn to unlearn the habit of blaming others by taking full responsibility for our thought speech and action. Habit Editing and TSA Alignment will definitely play a role in eradicating habits which are harmful to our quality of life. We can root out the weeds of negativity by being aware of their presence, and by cultivating virtues of gratitude and forgiveness.

Benefits of Thought Harvesting:

There are countless benefits of Thought Harvesting. We will highlight a few important ones for our discussion.

Thoughts are building blocks of Spirituality: - Just like atom is the basic building block of matter, thought is the basic building block of spirit. Every thought is a chip of spirit, and stirs awareness. Thus, constantly talking about a certain idea or a material thing you want to manifest, you are forking a way for its manifestation. Buddha the enlightened one declared "you are what you think all day along". Just like a farmer decides to harvest barley he selects the best seeds of barley, and prepare the ground properly, before sowing the seeds of barley. The same way as a part of habit editing, you decide the person whom you want to be, and start harvesting thoughts towards that goal. For example, you want to be healthier and attractive than you are today. You consciously cultivate the habit of healthy eating, healthy sleeping and practicing regular exercising at a local gym. You can also cultivate the habit of going to bed early, and get up thirty minutes early to practice your gratitude to make your life amazing. Thought harvesting is an art and anybody can practice it.

Thought harvesting is the first step towards manifestation: - Anything you want to see happen in your life it begins with thought harvesting. Really speaking thoughts are things, as they mature themselves to be manifested matter. Every thought is a disturbance in the ocean of consciousness and by cultivating desirable thoughts, you will be able to manage your own mind which is sum total of all your thoughts at any given time. You chose your thoughts by harvesting them, and soon you will be on your way to weave your own experience in life. Your thoughts, manufacture your emotions, and your emotions dictate your state of mind, which is who you are. If your thoughts are harmonious, your emotions are uplifting like love and compassion. If your thoughts are wrapped up in negativity causing disturbances, your emotions like resentment, anger and violence emerge to torpedo your peace of mind. You will behave like a helpless wooden plank caught up in the high seas.

So deliberately think about the thoughts you want to harvest, like love, kindness and gratitude that can make your life a meaningful voyage.

"As a man thinketh in his heart, so is he "declares the Old Testament. Cultivate calming thoughts to evolve into a creative thinker and manifest any material things you like to have. Thought is the most powerful tool every human being has at his or her disposal even though we seldom realize it.

Thought harvesting is mind harvesting. When thoughts grow without conscious harvesting it is like a jungle the habitat for wild animals like lion, tiger, elephant or venomous snakes. The same way an uncultured mind is the habitat for emotional tigers, elephants and lions appearing to us like rage, anger, resentment and frustration. Thought harvesting helps us clear the mental weeds of emotional ups and downs that can be triggered by external forces beyond our control. As a matter of fact, Thought Harvesting is one step in the practice of emotional hygiene, which promote emotional freedom stemming from vibrant emotional health. We all talk about political freedom and economic freedom — period, and nobody talks about (very seldom people) emotional freedom where one is free of emotional slavery. Really speaking, the economic freedom and political freedom we are unable to enjoy without emotional freedom, where our ego is well contained and the mind is curious and creative enough to weave new fabrics of imagination, the most Godlike quality we are all endowed with. Unless we harmonize our animal nature, and enhance our own will power, life on earth will be wasted in the pursuit of delusion. Thought harvesting enables us to remove the clutters of negativity from the landscape of our mental sphere and bring forth the much-needed clarity and harmony.

Thought Harvesting is Emotional Hygiene:

Thought Harvesting is an integral part of emotional hygiene which is the foundation of mental health. Just like we follow the rules of physical hygiene to maintain robust health and wellbeing we need to practice daily the rituals of emotional hygiene to maintain emotional health which is essential for our success and happiness in life. Just like our physical body is an instrument of expression our mind is our instrument of perception, enabling us to perceive the world around us. Our five sense organs are the perceptual agents of our mind. They facilitate to and fro communications with our areas of our brain the ultimate command and control center. Habit editing and thought harvesting keep the engine of emotional hygiene running smoothly even when emotions run high and overwhelming. Without thought harvesting, thoughts run wild and out of control causing our animal instinct to overtake the human instinct. During our childhood our parents do the thought harvesting for us. Mothers play a great role in helping us choose our thoughts constantly reminding of what to think and what not to think. They point out the thoughts we must plant on a daily basis and practice thoughts until they become habits.

Thought Harvesting is Habit formation:

Our life is nothing but a parade of habits, those seemingly insignificant rituals we repeat day in and day out. Even the

American President brushes his teeth, just like his mother taught him, decades ago when he was a three-year-old child. The basic skill of brushing the teeth even if he went to Harvard, and did law school there remains the same. Those automatic repetition of rituals what we learned from our mother still remain the same regardless of who we have become or what profession we choose to practice. The thoughts of respecting our parents, teachers, and elders have become our shadows of behavior throughout our adult life. It is easier to harvest thoughts during our formative years as we follow the instructions from our parents, and also in many cases we also emulate our older siblings. I still remember a habit of respecting elders who may be just older than me like an uncle or friends' father or an older brother or sister. If we are sitting when they enter the room, we stand up as a mark of respect and sit down only after the elders grab their seats. I still remember my mother when I do that because, she insisted that we children do that as a mark of respect to elders. Surprisingly when we do that, everybody in the room follows that custom. Even today at the age of eighty, when my boss comes into my office, I stand up as a mark of respect to her, though she is decades younger than me. No wonder, somebody declared "habit is a merciless master". If habit is a merciless master, we need to be the slaves of a good master, who can imbibe in us healthy and harmonious rituals of daily practice. I cannot thank my mother enough in inculcating good habit in me at a very young age, like any other mother, and it has tremendously helped me to become a Gratitude Practitioner. We all need to bow before our parents' wisdom, especially we bow before the sacrifices of our mothers.

Thought harvesting is only one aspect of our quest for transformation. The other two tools of engagement namely speech and action also need to be harvested to complete our total personal transformation. We deal with speech harvesting and deed harvesting in the pages that follow. The power of gratitude lies in enameling all our tools of engagement with respect appreciation, empathy, kindness and compassion.

How Speech and Action Transform you?

"Life and death are in the power of the tongue": New Testament

While thoughts are invisible, the words we express are nothing but display of our thoughts in open, and they, are audible and hence they are visible too. In the beginning there was word, word was with God, and the word was God. The power of God to create the manifested world, the seeable, touchable and feelable reality is embedded in the power of speech. The words are the elements of speech that hold in its womb, the form we want to manifest in the material world. After thought, the second most powerful tool of engagement with the universes is the speech, that can transform you from a sinner to a saint and vice versa. After all, the sinner and a saint can be identified by the speech they utter, that form of expressions that represent the invisible thoughts they hold in the secrecy of their mind. While the sinner is mired in negativity in the use of speech as a medium of communication, the saint is always exuberating enthusiasm and every word he or she utters is filled with hope and optimism. While the very nature of human life is pulsating with uncertainties, hope and optimism are the guide posts that lead to one's destiny, the chosen destination in one's life. Generally, we mine the thoughts in the incubator of our mind, many times the continuous expression of inspiring words help us germinate inspiring thoughts as a way of life.

Books that changed my life!

More than four decades ago, when I was searching for answers to my life's problems that culminated in financial losses, and loss of peace of mind I took refuge in many inspirational books and scriptures like Bhagvad Gita, New Testament and Holy Q'uran. Books like As a man thinketh, Power of positive thinking, power of your subconscious mind, How to win friends and influence people, have been my constant companions and close personal friends who ceaselessly inspired me and continue to inspire me even today. Some of the great one lines that perk me up today are as follow:

Love thy neighbor as thyself

When God is with you who could be against you?

This too shall pass?

Whatsoever Ye shall pray and ask for, believe ye have received ye shall receive.

Do your duty renouncing the fruit of action, when challenged by any problems in life.

Trust in Allah! But tie your camel!

Honor thy parents!

Remember two things, forget two things. Remember all the good things others have done for you. Remember God and your parents. Forget all the good things you have done for others, forget all the bad things others have done to you!

There are no accidents in the Universe!

The amount of happiness you derive in this world is directly proportionate to the amount of happiness you are willing to give others.

If you do not manage your mind, somebody else will mismanage it for you!

Nobody can completely escape the wrath of one's Karma (Your thoughts, speech and action)

Gratitude must be the only attitude in life.

God is everywhere and in everything.

The law of 'Reciprocity governs the Universe".

With God all things are possible.

Always put your mother next to God! (In fact, mother is God, as there will be no God, without a mother)

May there be peace and tranquility among all beings in the Universe.

Every organism is a complex of body, mind (instinct) and awareness.

Treat others the way you like to be treated!

In the interest of space, I have only quoted here the ones that serve as my teacher in my everyday life. I do not claim that I display exuberant optimism in all my dealings with the universe. But more than ninety percent of the time, and ninety percent of my transactions with the universe, I am able to court optimism and whenever I get discouraged, I notice my plight and bounce back to the territory of hope and encouragement. Whenever I am overwhelmed my negative emotions like loneliness in the absence of my spouse, I press into action my Emotional Circuit Breaker, that can halt the flow of negativity to my emotional state. This has been a wonderful tool for my emotional management. It is very difficult almost impossible to manage your emotions under all circumstances unless you are a Buddha, Jesus Christ or Krishna. The weakness of a mortal always follows us like a shadow, unless we are prepared to press into action our remedial tools like Emotional Circuit Breaker, and TSA alignment.

Choose Words and Expressions:

Our speech is an integral part of our communication, the words we speak and the tone in which they are expressed dictate the effectiveness of our daily communication. The expression that we use can imply politeness or rudeness, humility or arrogance. My mother always used to tell me when I was a teenager "Gopi you only use words to uplift others, and never to put down another person, regardless of how the other person behaves towards you". She also added that "if you cannot say something good about the other person, keep your mouth shut". Nobody will criticize you for what you did not say". Even though she had only fifth grade formal schooling, she was a master communicator as she was able to empathize with others, no matter from what background they came.

When you choose words and expression for everyday communication you do not become a scapegoat of other people's rudeness or arrogance. Your impulses are in check, and your selected words and expressions will follow in your communication journey. Even the use of derogatory expressions, slangs and the abusive four-letter words become Greek and Latin to you, as your habit of communication is formed and formatted with the civility and decency it very much deserves. To show the power of positive habits, I can vouch touching my heart that in the last fifty-two years living in America I never used the four-letter word even once. It is not an expression of arrogance, but point out the power of habit in each one of us. I can never imagine the use of four-letter words when I talk to my own wife and children let alone my friends, colleagues and clients. Almost all of us are creatures of habits and the words and expressions we use in our everyday communication is not an exception to the dominant habits. No matter who we are in our personal corporate or social life it is a very prudent idea to sanitize our own vocabulary. Vocabulary, being an integral part of our communication can help us in our personal transformation. Always remember that you will not be criticized for what you did not say as my mother would have reminded me almost seven decades ago. It is a very good idea to look at your habit of speech harvesting as a part of your own personal transformation. After more than five decades I am only happy that I sanitized my vocabulary that does not include any abusive or insulting expression, no matter what the other person is harping on. Transformation is all about being aware of your thought, speech and action the three tools of engagement we all have to interact with the universe!

Deed Harvesting:

Once Lord Rama, an incarnation of Hindu God Vishnu asked his spiritual teacher Vasishta "Oh!" revered one, what is punya (a good deed) and what is 'papa' (a sinful deed)? There came the answer, 'Rama deeds that heal are punya, and the deeds that hurt are 'papa'. Yes indeed. Just like there are uplifting words, and putting down words, there are also uplifting (healing) deeds and dangerous (hurting) deeds. Our action must at all times be righteous action, the one that uplifts another mortal on this planet. We are all here for a short journey, and we all without exception live in a borrowed body, with borrowed time. This body in which we live has come from the food and it will go back to food. No matter how healthy we keep the body, it has only certain amount of shell- life (or cell life), and it will disintegrate. This is not to discourage anyone from taking care of the body and its inducer mind, but to awaken to the truth that we are all mortal as long as we are encased in our body.

Deed harvesting not only sharpens our mind and body, it also helps us to distribute the awareness, for the optimal health of our body and mind. I am giving below a few deeds we can try to harvest in our daily life:

(1) Ten acts of kindness:

Hold the door for weak and the elderly, even better to one and all.

You can work in a soup kitchen, or if are hard pressed for time, you can support a favorite charity.

Cultivate a captivating smile to unleash on every one who crosses year path.

Find five minutes for your spouse, child or friends who need to take something out of their chest. (Do not try to give any advice during this precious time).

Give a small donation to a homeless man without judging him or her. This act of kindness reminds you how fortunate you are in the game of life.

Be kind to your spouse and children. They are the backbone of your existence. They give a meaning and purpose to your life.

Be kind to your coworkers and colleagues. In your capacity, even if you have to lay off some employees, be kind to them and do everything in your power to make the transition smooth and pain-free. Be a human being under all circumstances.

Wherever you find darkness, light up a candle without criticizing who is responsible for the darkness.

Call your parents at least once a week, or more and tell them how much you appreciate what they did for you.

If you have children attending college, call them occasionally and tell them 'I love you'.

These are small deeds that make a big difference. Come to think of it there are no big deeds in life only small deeds that make a big difference. Deed harvesting, like speech harvesting and thought harvesting is a 'life long process, and it is the process of personal transformation. Life is a journey without destinations and the joy is in the journey. Everyday thought speech and action add spice to life. Life is like Netflix a streaming experience. You alone can decide what types of episodes you are streaming every day. Your thoughts speech and action add color and substance to your streaming experience

CHAPTER XI

HOW CAN YOU CHANGE YOUR PARADIGM?

THOUGHT TRANSFORMATION!

Almost all motivational speakers, spiritual leaders, and social media experts talk about a paradigm shift as a panacea for all human problems, whether they are financial problems, relationship issues, or health challenges. Yet very seldom do these pundits suggest concrete steps that lead to a paradigm shift. But before we suggest concrete measures one can take to reverse the paradigm, we need to understand the concept and its implications in personal life. Definitely a change in paradigm or the sum total of one's belief system has innumerable benefits in everyday life. It is like changing the lenses on one's glasses for better vision. In this case, it is one's world vision.

WHAT IS A PARADIGM?

The word paradigm comes from the Greek word 'paradeigma' which means a pattern, method or system. In a scientific sense, it means a clear set of concepts, patterns or postulates used in research fields. There is always a controversy between physical scientists and social scientists about the use of paradigm shift. Regardless of what the Physical scientists say, the term paradigm is very popular with social scientists and thought leaders, motivational speakers, and corporate trainers. It has become a very popular term most people like to include in their everyday vocabulary.

The word has profound meaning with far reaching spiritual tentacles as it encompasses the entire system of one's belief. It represents the accumulated habits, rituals and practices that define who we are beneath our skin. It is influenced by our early childhood, the teachings of our parents, teachers and elders. The culture and customs we grew up with also equally contribute to our paradigm. If you think you can change that accumulated tendencies in the blink of an eye, it is an impossible task. Although those elements that define who we are and how we look at this world are not set in stone, we need to allow enough time to rewire our brains with new thoughts, speech and deeds. Once you have changed your paradigm which enhances your physical, emotional, and spiritual wellbeing, you can continue to follow it for the rest of your life. Like the Chinese proverb declares: "a journey of a thousand miles begins with a simple step". You must take that simple step today to change your paradigm for a better tomorrow.

I started my journey of transformation more than four decades ago, peeling off the old tendencies and simultaneously sowing the seeds of change. The toughest challenge one faces in this world-is changing oneself. After four decades of incremental changes, I need to confess that there is still a long way to go. I have embraced it as work in progress and will continue to practice until the last day on this planet.

You can embark on this journey of transformation, or paradigm shift by taking the following steps:

STEP ONE: THOUGHT HARVESTING.

Thought harvesting is the art of consciously planting new thoughts. Everything you want to do begins with a deep-rooted thought stemming from an intent. Every thought is a spiritual chip and you can deliberately create them or harvest them in the incubator of your consciousness. Thought harvesting is an art as well as a science. You become better and better by practicing it daily like a ritual. You also learn about the science of thinking and understanding the difference between thought, mind and awareness. You are a body, mind and awareness complex working in harmony to lead a well balanced life. While every thought can be compared to a drop of water, mind itself is like the Pacific Ocean with a surface and unfathomable depth. Since original thinking is time consuming and painful, we unconsciously leave it for others to think for us.. It is better to think for ourselves, regardless of who thinks, we are the ultimate victims or beneficiaries of those thoughts. One of the best ways of thought harvesting is reading Inspiration Books. When we read those books, we not only become familiar with the authors' thoughts, but those thoughts act as a catalyst to create new thoughts in us. This is the simplest method of thought harvesting with innumerable benefits. The great inventor Thomas Alva Edison used to say: "Ideas are in the Air". Thomas Edison was one of the great Thought Harvesters, who had more than thousand patents to his credit. The great inventors, artists, writers and comedians are great thought harvesters as they burn spiritual oil to produce new thoughts. Almost all of the human beings do thought harvesting, many times without realizing it. You can select a few books like New Testament, Old Testament, Bhagavad Gita, Holy Quran Talmud, and other scriptures of various traditions. They all contain pearls of wisdom for us to grasp and practice. You will get best results by reading them more than once. Every time you read you have a different perspective and a new meaning. That is why our parents and grandparents recommend reading at least a passage from the scriptures daily. It will open up vistas of possibilities and our own potential. Besides the holy Scriptures I recommend the following books that helped me when I was challenged by the vicissitudes of life:

1..As a Man Thinketh

2. How to win friends and Influence People

3. The Power of Your Subconscious Mind

4. Think and Grow Rich

5. Edenborough Lectures on Mental Science

6.The Power of Now

7. Heart of Awareness

8.Yoga Sutras by Pathanjali

9.Manage Your Mind, Manage your Life

10. Gopi's Gratitude Journal

11. Autobiography of a Yogi

STEP: TWO

Write Down Positive Thoughts Daily

When you read a book, especially an inspirational one you come across a number of positive thoughts and ideas. You can write them down in a notebook and loudly recite them. I still remember more than four decades ago, when I was reading New Testament, I wrote down several times "When God is with you, who could be against you?" The profundity of that positive declaration from the Lord Jesus Christ is still ringing in my years. I use the positive message constantly when challenged by day today problems, especially when they seem to be impossible to overcome. I also suggest that powerful message to my friends when they approach me with their problems. Surely, it is a God given message timeless, and anybody can use it regardless of race, religion, or color of the skin. Writing a message daily will have a lasting effect on your memory, and that act can rewire your brain as the modern neuroscientists have discovered. "The neurons that fire together, wire together" declare the brain experts, as they witness that physical and biochemical changes under the microscope and a fMRI. When you recite them as you write them daily, it fortifies retention and long term memory. This simple daily practice will help without your knowledge to modify your own belief system.

STEP THREE: PRACTICE GRATITUDE:

Gratitude is more than a virtue. In fact it is a way of life. We consciously try to look at the Universe through the prism of gratitude. When I was growing up in a small village in the South Indian State of Kerala, my mother always used to tell me "Gopi, whatever God gives you (whatever challenges you face), accept them with both hands, and say thank you, It could have been worse." I have used her words of wisdom whenever I was challenged even with seemingly heart breaking problems. That attitude of gratitude in facing any problem in life has helped me all the time, to regain my calmness and clarity.

Yesterday ended with last night.

Intellectually we all understand that yesterday ended with

last night. Yet we are all emotionally clinging to the past like a leech, never letting go of the past pain, frustration and ridicule completely. Yesterday ended with last night, as all events in life are fleeting. Time is like a river. The river that you stepped in at this moment is no longer there, as it is flowing without tracing its past. Our yesterdays however painful they were, disappeared behind the curtain of time. Today is a new dawn, and you can capture it with more vigor and enthusiasm, and accomplish anything you want to accomplish. Your Gratitude Journal is not only the beginning of your new dawn, it redefines your life, and paves way for a new beginning. Anything well begun is half done, said the famous Greek Philosopher Plato. Thus away from the yesterday of failed attempts, despair and discouragement you are starting a new day of hope, optimism and higher vibrations. Things happen in life both pleasant and unpleasant. It is unavoidable. If you are happy you are bound to be unhappy as both happiness and unhappiness exist in the field of time. Anything attached to the wheel of time is fleeting, and you can not expect those experiences to stand still. The most important thing in life is not what happens to you, but how you respond to those events. Practice of Gratitude helps to respond to every event appropriately, instead of reacting to it irrationally. Gratitude helps you remain in the present moment, without vacillating towards the past or vexing about the uncertainties of the future. Practice of Gratitude heals, it is your catalyst, that transformative agent who can help you rewrite your destiny.

GRATITUDE AFFIRMATIONS!

I am grateful to the Universe!

I am grateful to the Universe!

I am grateful to the Universe!

(PLEASE READ ALOUD)

BENEFITS OF PRACTICING GRATITUDE:

1. Gratitude is the source (mother) of all positive emotions.
2. Gratitude heals both the physical and emotional wounds!
3. Gratitude erases negativity from the shores of human mind!
4. Gratitude is antidote for all fears!

5. Gratitude puts out the flames of anger!

6. Gratitude cultivates Compassion!

7. Gratitude promotes appreciation for everything!

8. Gratitude produces endorphins in the body!

9. Gratitude cultivates respect for every one and everything.
10. Gratitude is the greatest attitude towards life!

ANATOMY OF GRATITUDE:

G(Generosity.: Generosity is another name for open ended approach to life. Gratitude demands open-mindedness and transferable transparency. It removes completely the attitude of my way or the highway. The very act of expressing gratitude is a testimony to the openness of the individual towards life.

R:RESPECT: Respect is the heartbeat of gratitude. One of the most misunderstood words in the English language is respect. We all say I respect my parents, I respect my teachers, and what is more to talk about respect. We must respect parents, teachers, elders, strangers, enemies (if you have), and even a homeless person. We must respect our spouses, children and everyone who comes across our path. Respect is holding in high esteem others regardless of who they are and what they do. Respect defines a line of dignity that we will not cross under any circumstances, even if the other person does not show respect towards us. If you do not treat others with respect, you are crossing the line of dignity which does not define the other person but says everything about you. Once you start practicing gratitude, you begin to respect others regardless of who they are.

A:ATTITUDE: Gratitude is an attitude, the ultimate attitude that defines your character, and it can keep negativity in check under all circumstances. Your attitude, general outlook, and worldview can decide your altitude-how high you will go in life at the personal, professional, and social levels. One of the outstanding traits of the human mind is that it is coachable, teachable, and amenable to suggestions. Practice of Gratitude is a teaching tool for all of us to train our minds to be a positive, and grateful mind. With the practice of Gratitude, you will open the floodgates of opportunities that will remain closed for you otherwise.

T:TRAINING: Gratitude is a positive training. It can teach the skill of emotional vibrancy and empathy. It teaches us to regulate our emotions even under trying circumstances. You manage your emotions well, without being angry and instead of reacting you will learn to respond to the situation. When emotions run high at home, or at the place of work a gratitude practitioner is able to contain his or her ego, bringing down the temperature in the room. This training is an invisible training, aftermath of daily practice, and the transformative effect of gratitude. He does not need to bite his tongue under trying circumstances, as the tongue is well harnessed to stay quiet.

I:INTEGRITY: Integrity is an essential purpose of Gratitude Practice. You are true to yourself, you abandon the hypocrisy, as you become transparent. A grateful person is a peaceful person and his or her transparency becomes obvious. His Thought Speech and Action are in alignment almost all the time as a result of intense training and noble intentions. Personal integrity is the alpha and omega of one's character. Ultimately character is the currency of Trust, which we all need to accomplish anything worthwhile in this world with the help of others. It does not matter whether you are a politician, business leader, or an entrepreneur or an academician, we all need to enjoy the trust of others. While diplomacy could be marginally sugar coating, personal integrity is the heart of building trust. Practice of Gratitude is the pathway to building trust.

T:TENACITY: Tenacity is an essential ingredient of Gratitude. Gratitude is a core value we have to pursue for years, and lasts a life time. Why so? Gratitude is a way of life, transcending as it enters the portico of eternity. Even after the body has disintegrated as everybody will eventually, the person's character encased in Gratitude lives on as long as time endures. Gratitude for great souls like Mahatma Gandhi, Martin Luther King Jr, or Mother Theresa endures even after their mortal frames have disappeared into eternity. Once you start practicing Gratitude, it becomes your lifestyle, and it follows you like a shadow wherever you go. The element of Tenacity keeps you focused in the present moment in spite of external distractions and influences.

U:UNDERSTANDING: Gratitude is understanding. The purpose of life is to serve others, and the first step towards the service is remembering what contributions others have made to make you who you are. You understand the sacrifices made by your parents, teachers elders, and others who belonged to the extended family. From a deep understanding of the roles others have played in your life, you can not help but being grateful to them. It is worthwhile to mention the roles your spouse and children have played in your life although they joined the journey later in your life.

Practice of Gratitude also promotes understanding between human beings. Empathy is the tributary of gratitude. Instead of sympathizing with others, you empathize with others by stepping into their shoes to understand their struggles, challenges and emotions. Once you understand and evaluate your own feelings and emotions, it will be easier for you to empathize with others. You will listen to them more, to know what troubles and tribulations they are going through. This understanding helps you to eliminate the tendency to judge others for their reactions and behaviors. Misunderstanding is not in the dictionary of a grateful person.

D: Divinity: Gratitude is the embodiment of Divinity. It is said that the "hand that gives is the hand of God! In all religious traditions the need for gratitude is emphasized. In his letter to Thessalonians, St.Paul wrote: "En Panti Eucharisteite", which translated from Greek means in everything gives thanks. "Be grateful under all circumstances", apostle Paul declared. Be aware of everything that happens in your life," accepts them and give thanks, it could have been worse" as my mother used to tell me.

ENERGY: Gratitude is energy, it is the playground of Awareness. As we all know energy can not be created, it can not be destroyed, but it can be transformed. Practice of Gratitude creates high vibrational energy. To test this point, when you are feeling dull, or bored write a "Gratus Card" to your friend or anybody for that matter and observe your own energy level. You will feel better as your energy is ascending towards higher echelons. Practice of Gratitude, like meditation can change your energy level to embrace noble aspirations and higher values in life Gratitude is divine! When you express gratitude, you are passing your positive energy to the other. Gratitude instantly creates two winners, the giver as well as the receiver. Many precious moments of expressing gratitude lasts a life time. When I was growing up my mother used to tell me" Gopi if you eat food, it will last for twenty four hours, but if you give that food to another hungry person, it will last a life time. Even though her wisdom was so deep for me to understand, I now understand what she meant. The divine energy of gratitude has far reaching spiritual tentacles that can transform you to be a harmonious person in all areas of life. That is why it is said:

A grateful person is a peaceful person

A grateful family is a peaceful family

A grateful community is a peaceful community

A grateful country is a peaceful country

A grateful world is a peaceful world.

It is very clear that Gratitude is energy, and it is a conduit of peace wherever is appears.

STEP:FOUR EMOTIONAL BALANCING

Emotional imbalance is on an increase at an alarming rate, as the foundation of emotional strength is collapsing due to our inability to balance emotions. Every emotion is created due to intense mental activities, and it is expressed in the body like anger, frustration, fear anxiety, and in extreme cases suicidal tendencies. If you do not handle the emotional imbalance on a regular basis, it can lead to an onset of mental and physical ailments. The very nature of the emotional imbalance is its unpredictability. So all of us must watch the emotional upheavals from the very beginning, even it does not appear to be serious. Just like a weatherman observes atmospheric changes to predict severe weather conditions like a tornado, severe thunder storms, lightening or even a Tsunami, we all need to observe mental changes especially creeping negativity and anger and depression or even slight feeling of helplessness. Negative emotions accumulated over a period of time can cause emotional imbalance that can threaten our personal well-being.

You can not look for a fire extinguisher when the house is on fire. You need to keep one at home, in case the house catches on fire. You must anticipate stressful situations that could arise in the future and take remedial steps to tackle that effectively. For example you have an important presentation coming for senior leaders of the company including the CEO who is flying from New York. You need to have talk about it with your spouse and children. This will help them to help you navigate through the stressful time. They could also cheer lead you to keep you positive and focused. Your family will cooperate with you by handling small chores without getting you involved. The same way, you need to let your boss know that your wife is having major surgery in the next two weeks. This will enable her to keep your workload low, and give you a few days off on medical leave or pto. These simple examples show small preparations can save you lot of emotional turmoil either at home or at work. Proper communication and planning along with awareness are the key to reducing emotional imbalance in daily life.

Of course if things get out of control, do not wait until you break down. Instead, resort to early intervention by seeking the help of a psychologist or a therapist. You must discuss the problem of unmanaged stress level with your spouse and adult children. One thing to remember is that nobody can really help you like you yourself. You only know what is going on in your mind, and how it is impairing your ability to function as a normal human being.

Keeping physical and emotional well-being is a work in progress and every day must be utilized to make even incremental changes. Taking care of your body and mind is an essential activity that you can not delegate to your own spouse. Some of the basic rituals (daily tasks) you must incorporate in your daily" Love To Do List" are as follows:

1. Take your eating habits seriously.

2. Take your sleeping habits seriously.

3. Go to work out/Gym regularly

4. Have some spiritual activities regularly like going to a place of worship, mindful meditation, reading, writing, and quiet time for at least fifteen minutes

5. Have a physical exam at least once a year.

STEP NUMBER FIVE: USE IMAGINATION DAILY

Imagination is the most God-like quality in man. Man is created in the image and likeness of God. When we were small children, we could imagine being anyone we wanted to be. We could imagine being a bird, a butterfly or even an angel. There is no logic in imagination, simply curiosity wrapped in emotion. As we grow into adulthood, we lose our grip on curiosity as we think logically and reasoning many a time becomes an impediment to our own growth. But imagination removes the inhibition from our thought process, and we become free from the weight of logic. As adults, we must continue to be curious and spread our wings of imagination like a bird in the blue sky of ambition and dreams to realize our full potential. We all have hidden potential waiting to be awakened with a touch of imagination.

Great Luminaries of Imagination:

Wright Brothers: When the creative Wright Brothers dreamed of flying in the air, they made a prototype of an airplane. But their first model of air plane lasted less than a minute in the air. But today when we travel for fourteen or seventeen hours to get from one corner of the earth to the farthest corner we do not even think about the Wright Brothers and their imaginative faculty in designing an airplane. The flying palaces of today designed and manufactured by Boeing and Air Bus were the result of the imagination of the Wright Brothers. An unemployed painter in despair, living on top of a garage simply scribbled the picture of a mouse, that revolutionized the playground and theme parks of millions of children and adults all over the world. That painter who managed to survive on top of a garage infested with mice was none other than Walt Disney. Disney World is one of the best theme parks in the world attracting millions of children and adults. In our own time, there is a living example of a writer named J.K. Rowling, who imagined a ten-year-old boy by the name of Harry Porter, as a figment of her wild imagination. Twelve publishers rejected Harry Porter's story before one publisher accepted the book for publication. Now the fruits of J.K. Rowling's wildest imagination is enjoyed by millions of teen agers all over the world. J.K.Rowling herself did very well in the process by making over a billion dollars, in addition to her name and fame. She has changed the world of writing and imagination through her imaginary character of Harry Potter. Imagination can not only change your paradigm, it can change the paradigm of society and even the world itself. J.K.Rowling through her imaginary character Harry Potter, has become an immortal story teller who will live through generations to come.

IMAGINATION AND VISUALIZATION.

The landscape of imagination is far and wide, and it can be applied at the micro level. Visualization is a technique of imagination at the micro level where every individual applies the specific technique to accomplish his or her own individual dreams. While imagination is like a wild forest, visualization is at the individual level, to focus on a specified goal. Visualization is a time-tested technique to practice creating mental images on a daily basis. While anybody can use the technique of visualization to accomplish any seemingly impossible goals, famous athletes like Michael Phelps the Olympian Swimmer and winner of a record number of gold medals, has used the technique of visualization. As a young swimmer Michael had trouble focusing, until he came to Coach Bob Bowman. He started by teaching Michael to learn relaxation techniques. It is necessary to relax before you can visualize as a prattling mind can not focus. Michael became the best in visualization techniques before every swim competition whether at the national level or in the Olympics. No matter how hard you practice your skills, anything can go wrong at the last moment. The delay in starting the competition, minor physical problems, or even mental disturbances due to external factors. In Michaels own words "Any small thing could go wrong. I am ready". Visualization is a time-tested practice to harness the powers of the subconscious mind. Even the great teacher of Mental Science declared "Whatsoever ye shall pray and ask for, believe ye have received, ye shall receive". Modern research in Neuro Science has discovered that neurons in the brain will move, whether you are doing physical training or mental training. In other words, there is no difference between imagining a task as done, or physically doing it. In Mental Science we say that the subconscious mind does not know the difference between a synthetic experience or actual experience.

My personal experience with Visualization. After studying about the power of the Sub conscious mind and the power of visualization in harnessing the Subconscious mind, I wanted to experiment with it. I am a firm believer in taking action. It was 1985, and as a young man I wanted to have a Mercedes Benz car. I started visualizing the car in minute detail, the color, the sunroof and above all the Mercedes emblem on the car. I imagined that I was driving the car with my wife sitting next to me in the open car. All three boys were sitting in the back seat and giggling. I could feel my wife's hair in the breeze flying and touching my cheeks. The humming sound of the air conditioner, and the giggling sound of the kids and my own ecstatic feeling were alive and real. I used to visualize this drive in my living room everyday as soon as I wake up and before going to sleep. One of the effective techniques is to visualize at dawn and just before going to sleep since the conscious mind is in a state of semi-waking state. When that happens, the subconscious mind is in a state of peak alert, ready to absorb anything that you choose to impress upon it. No wonder, this is the best time most of the religious traditions chosen as an appropriate time suitable for prayer. I kept on doing it every day, and by April of 1986 started, I got a call from a good friend of mine who was moving back to India. He had a Mercedes car he wanted to give to me. He did not ask for any money, as he simply wanted to give it to me, although there were other people who really wanted it. I got the Car and of course, I paid him a reasonable price. That is beside the point. This experiment taught me two things: Anything is possible if you visualize diligently without questioning the logic behind it. Second, you must believe in the effectiveness of the technique of visualization.

In conclusion, all these simple practices are daily rituals that can rewire your brain to change your paradigm. "The neurons that fire together, wire together" is a scientifically proven statement. You are a vibrant body, a sharp mind, powered by unfathomable awareness with spiritual tentacles spread all across the Universe. Therefore it is said poetically that every thought creates a ripple in the ocean of consciousness. Thus these three vital elements, inseparable, make you the Whole person, why even the holy person. In the absence of any of these three vital elements, you cease to be that whole person, incapable of leading a purposeful life in the world. Your beautiful body has a certain shell life, and at the end it is destined to disintegrate. This disintegration of the body is commonly known as death. Knowing death as an integral part of life reduces our sorrow when a dear one departs from the world. Really speaking we are all living in a borrowed body, with borrowed time. Every day is a celebration of life. Every day is indeed a blessing! That is why practicing Gratitude is essential, which enables us to live in the present moment. To enhance our paradigm keep asking the question: WHO AM I?

CHAPTER XII

The Law of Reciprocity

"There are no accidents, whatsoever, in the Universe". Ram Dass.

I got married to The Law of Reciprocity sometime in 2014. I have no recollection of where I read about, but it has been a spiritual eye-opener for me. But based on whatever I learned about it. I was able to define The Law of Reciprocity as follows:

"The Law of Reciprocity says whatever you offer to the Universe, it will come back to you multiplied".

There are only three ways we can offer anything to the universe, namely our thoughts, our speech, and our action. Every thought is a chip from the spirit, the most powerful energy in the universe. A thought is defined as a mental image, an idea, a construct or an abstract that is capable of manifestation in the right environment. All great achievements of humanity began with a simple idea or a thought, and then it manifested itself in the physical form. The simple mental image dawned on the thinker that manifested itself into a monument or memorial or a huge stadium or a famous temple or a place of worship. The iconic Taj Mahal, that was erected in 1632 was an idea or thought in the mind of the fifth Mughal Emperor Shah Jahan. He created a one-of-a-kind illumined Colosseum in memory of his thirteenth wife Mumtaz Mahal, who died during childbirth to their fourteenth child. The pain of grief struck him so much, that he needed to do something that no mortal ever did.

Similarly, the incandescent light bulb was just a thought in the mind of Thomas Alva Edison. Despite his repeated failures over a thousand times, Edison held on to his idea or dream until it manifested as a light bulb that he originally visualized on his mental screen. Every thought, according to the Indian philosophy of Vedanta, creates a ripple in the ocean of consciousness, and it gathers spiritual momentum before it can manifest itself into its material equivalent. There is a cause-and-effect relationship between thought and its material form, which can be called its effect. Every effect is the result of a cause. When you remove the cause from the effect, nothing remains. Thoughts can be voluntary or involuntary, and most of the thoughts are voluntary. Involuntary thoughts are premeditated ones, as you are contemplating about building something. For example, if you want to build a house for yourself. You will think about the place you want to build, and the details of the home like the number of bedrooms, bathrooms etc. before you talk to an architect to create a blueprint for your home. You are entertaining a parade of thoughts, and most of them were generated as a part of your planning to build a home for your family.

The famous Harry Potter character was just an idea in the mind of its famous author, J. K. Rowling. The idea germinated in her mind while she was travelling from Manchester to London. Even J.K. Rowling was rejected by twelve publishers before the thirteenth publishers picked it up for publishing. The only reason the thirteenth publisher agreed to publish, is because his eight-year-old daughter liked the story. J.K. Rowling was an unknown writer and most of the publishers are unwilling to bet on an unknown author, that could result in a financial loss. But the idea of Harry Potter was a billion-dollar idea as she generated above billion dollars, and J.K. Rowling broke all the records in the publishing industry based on the revenue it generated for her as its author. The Harry potter hysteria spread like a wildfire in the minds of teenagers, all over the world, that even Hollywood wanted to be a part of the Harry Potter Story.

Just like thoughts are offerings to the Universe, so are the speeches or the verbal expression one makes to the other. The mental images created in the mind can be expressed in words, or they can be written down like a book of prose or poetry. The oldest book of Vedas, in Hinduism, is nothing but hymns that originated in the mind of great Hindu seers who spent their lifetime looking for the truth about life. As a result of their years of contemplation, they had great mental images in the form of thoughts that they articulated in the form of Vedas for the world to read and understand. In the beginning those words were transmitted to their disciples by whispering, into their ears, and hence Vedas are also called Smritis, that which is heard. Finally, they were written down on palm leaves by the great seers, using a crude writing instrument for the benefit of mankind.

So. whatever we speak good or bad, noble, or vicious, is also an offering to the universe According to The Law of Reciprocity, whatever we offer as our speech will also be reciprocated in kind multiple times. It does not matter who said or what was said good or bad, noble or ennoble, it will come back manifold. It is said in the bible, in the beginning there was word; the word was with God: and the word was God". Every spoken word is a vortex of energy, it is capable of creation, and manifestation in, its physical form. Let us look at the word 'ABRACADABRA', which is uttered by every magician before he starts his show. There was research done at MIT about the origin of the word ABRACADABRA. They traced the origin of this word to Aramaic, the language that Lord Jesus Christ spoke. Interestingly, it means "I create as I speak". It shows the power of the spoken word. We all know the power of a spoken word with an orator like Cicero. Orators are the masters of swaying public opinion by the magical powers of the words they speak.

Even when we speak to a child, the word we speak will have a direct impact on the child. We can inspire a child, insult a child, or scare a child. Our mothers are magic makers when it comes into using the power of the spoken word. Many of the world leaders like Mahatma Gandhi, Abraham Lincoln, President Ronald Reagan talk about their great mother who instilled in them a sense of purpose, using simple words. Words coming out of a mother's mouth can convert even an ordinary mortal into an immortal whose name and deeds will endure as long as time endures. Once we understand the power of the spoken word, we will be very careful when we use them every day. My mother used to tell me "Gopi be very careful about what you speak. It can manifest it as reality in an emotionally charged moment. As a teenager, I did not understand the depth of my mother's thought or the profundity of her wisdom. But after brooding over it over decades, now I get the power of an emotionally charged word or words.

Then comes our own deeds or actions. The vortex of energy starting with our own thought, transformed into, and expressed in words, become the ultimate physical manifestation. In our example of J. K. Rowling, the character Harry Potter was simply a mental image when he landed on the mental plane of Ms. Rowling during her train journey from Manchester to

London. She started writing about Harry Potter in minute details, with hours and days and months and years of tireless research before the book Harry Potter was created in its manuscript form. It was rejected by twelve publishers before the thirteenth one decided to publish it and ultimately made J. K. Rowling became rich and famous and the reading world deeply indebted to her gift to mankind. Now it is a feelable, touchable, readable book the ultimate physical reality, which was merely a mental image, when it dawned in the mental tablet of J. K. Rowling. A literary feast of imagination, art and wisdom from a young and frustrated single mother who was once thinking about committing suicide because of her poverty and inability to make a living. Even when twelve publishers rejected her, she had the determination and grit to move forward to the thirteenth one who nodded and accepted the manuscript for publication.

The three tools of engagement

Thus, we human beings have been given three tools of engagement to communicate with the universe namely the thought, speech, and action. We are all using those tools constantly, regardless of who we are and where we are going with our life. A peasant or a king, an artist or a kingmaker, a writer, or a businessman, each one uses those tools of engagement in our everyday transaction with the universe. Our thoughts, speech and action are nothing but our own offering to the universe. The great physicist and genius Albert Einstein said that our universe is engulfed in energy which cannot be created or destroyed, yet it can be transformed. These are the three stages of converting energy into matter, namely the thought stage, speech stage, and the action stage. Many times, the process of conversion or transformation is incomplete, as unconsciously abated, if the three stages of transformation are not aligned. So, the alignment of thought, speech, and action (TSA) is an essential part of transformation. TSA alignment is also very essential for us to find our own inner peace, the lack of which creates an inner conflict which is the basis of almost all physical and mental ailments of mankind. We call every ailment a disease (not at ease, or at peace) which if not addressed at an early stage properly can threaten the very function of our body and mind which is very crucial for our happy living on the planet. We must understand the impact of The Law of Reciprocity on all aspects of our life, as we are all constantly interacting with the world outside, regardless of our race religion or the political affiliation. Our thoughts, speech and our action are our perennial messengers to the universe! Throughout our waking hours they are carrying our messages to the world outside, and the experience that we get out of the universe is manufactured by our very thoughts, speech, and action. This is the most difficult thing for all of us to digest. But that is the stark reality of life, that we are indeed the architect of our own destiny, whether we realize it or not.

"As above, so below

As within, so without!"

The above quote is from the world-famous Emerald Tablet, a tablet from antiquity declaring wisdom for human survival. It is said that our destiny is based on the thought that we entertain in the secret chambers of our own mind. Every intense thought we repeatedly think becomes a venerable vortex of energy capable of converting itself into its material equivalent. The Biblical saying that as a man thinketh in his heart, so is he points to the same mystical truth that indeed we are all the authors of our own book of life. Even though many of us get it at the intellectual level, but at the emotional level we seldom realize this truth and hence suffer the consequences.

The Blame Game

The blame game that is going on in this world is the living proof that emotionally we do not understand the truth that our own thought, speech and action conspire themselves to create our very experience that we conveniently ascribe to other people. This is how the blame game starts. For example, I can say that I am from a very "conservative Nair family and my mother was very strict, and the father never smiled, and my aunt and uncle seldom cared about me". While we could trace some truth in it, as children to a great extent are programmed by their parents, and the family they grow up with, we cannot continue to use it as a blame throughout our adult life as we are all capable of reprogramming our brain and our outlook. Our conclusion that our shortcomings are the results of our upbringing, or our parenting, is easy to accept as an excuse for our inadequacies. Basically, every blame game is a trick our own ego plays on us to shun its responsibility.

The blame game ultimately becomes embedded in our consciousness, that we will never be able to come out of it, unless we stop the blame game and accept full responsibility for our thoughts, speech, and action. The best solution of blame game is to be aware of our thoughts, particularly and replace all the negative thoughts that creep into our consciousness with positive and inspiring thoughts. Similarly, pay attention to the words that we choose in our everyday conversation. The same way, we look at our deeds that we do and examine them for their impact on other people, starting with our own family members. We can classify our deeds into hurting deeds and healing deeds, and stay focus on doing deeds that are beneficial to others. In the beginning, it is very difficult to change them, as our habits have a great grip on our thoughts speech and deeds. But we only look at the incremental changes, rather than colossal changes in a short period of time. Rome was not built in a day, so is our personality which is the accumulated sum of our thoughts, speeches and actions collected over our entire lifetime. But with discipline, Patience, and consistency, we all can bring satisfactory changes to our thoughts, speech and action in thirty days, sixty days, and ninety days.

AWARENESS TRAINING

Awareness training is the foundation of cultivating dominant thoughts, chosen speech and harmonious action. Just like any training, it requires a drill master one who can conduct daily drills, also called the repetition of practice, to ensure flawless performance. In awareness training, that drill master is called Will Power. Like any other habits, will power will be cultivated by repeated practices at regular intervals. There are no substitute for practice, as that alone can harness the power of the subconscious mind, that obedient servant of the conscious mind. The power of the subconscious transcends time and space capable of executing the command of the master, which is the logical thinking mind. It is the job of the objective mind to bring and focus awareness, the internal energy that cannot be created or destroyed, yet it can be transformed in any way we choose. Just like a potter creates a mold, for any type of pottery he wants to create, we all need to have a blueprint of a life we need to have before we start pouring our thoughts, speech, and action into the mold. Unfortunately, it does not happen most of the time, as we think, speak, and act any way we want without meditating about the consequences those thoughts, speech and action will bring forth. The Law of Reciprocity reminds you that unless we understand and apply this supreme universal law in all areas in life, we will float like a plank caught in the high seas going hither and thither. We will be devoting more time about the application of The Law of Reciprocity in later chapters.

We all can convert negative thoughts, speech, and action into their positive equivalents. Once we consciously start converting the negative thoughts into positive thoughts, the experience we create in the outer life will undergo radical changes. The same way, we can convert speeches and action into their positive equivalents too. These daily drills of consciously thinking, consciously speaking, and consciously acting, act like a spiritual platform for total transformation. With the help of the universal Law of Reciprocity and its application in our personal life we can radically transform other area of our life too, like relationship, personal careers, social and spiritual, influences.

Power of the spoken words

Words derive their power from the emotion with which they are uttered. Ancient Rishis of India used to curse when they were angry and grant boons when they were pleased. The bible makes it very clear" "life and death are in the power of the tongue". Both the curse and the boon are the direct reflection of the emotional power embedded in the words. Words are very ineffective if they are uttered without strong feeling or emotions, like in a monologue. Enlightened masters have developed their subconscious mind where the paranormal faculties reside.

Even Lord Jesus Christ himself has cursed a fig tree to be barren, and it became so. We must all understand the power of the spoken word, as it impacts others, and our own state of mind. It is a very good thought hygiene to watch our thoughts and watch our words so that unconscious utterances will not injure others. Unconscious thoughts also injure others, even though we seldom realize it, as thoughts are invisible and their effects we do not understand. Every thought in fact creates a ripple in the ocean of consciousness. The best way to eliminate negative thoughts and negative speech is to saturate your mental sphere with positive thoughts and positive speeches. You can think about doing things that will inspire others, help others in everyday life. With the weight of the positivity, negative thoughts and speech will drown. Just like the light swallows darkness, positivity reduces negativity if not eliminate it altogether.

All the social media, print media and T.V. are saturated with lot of negativities, as it has a special power to capture the attention of the audience, even though that negative news is detrimental to their emotional and physical wellbeing. We need to be positive and optimistic to successfully navigate through this world. The following story will further illustrate this point:

Once, certain creatures complained to the Sun God that there exists a place in the corner of the universe that is immersed in pitch darkness. The Sun God said, "I have not heard about such a place. If in fact it exists, I need to visit that place". Followed by the creatures, Sun God set out to that part of the universe enveloped in thick darkness. The creatures were surprised that all darkness vanished as soon as the Sun reached the place. We all know that darkness cannot exist in the presence of the sunlight. We must all carry our own sunlight of positive thoughts and positive words with us, and we will no more encounter dark conditions of despair despondency and disappointment in our lives.

Furthermore, we must always remember that just like a craftsman always keeps his tools in working condition at all times, we need to keep our tools of engagement with the universe in good condition. Our tools of engagement are our thoughts, our speech, and our action. We cannot use them effectively if they are rusty with negativity that dampens the sharpness of thought speech and our actions. When our life moves in the wrong direction, we blame other people including our parents, teachers, elders, the political system and even the creator, Himself, whom we accuse as being partial to people who are highly successful in their lives. It is easy to blame other people, rather than looking at our own thoughts, spoken words and the deeds that are harmful and hurtful to others. Surely the tragic state of blaming others will fade away, and we start paying attention to our thoughts, spoken words and the deeds, with awareness.

CHAPTER XIII

The Ultimate Thinking

The ultimate thinking is a thought in the form of a question -the answer to which eluded humanity from time immemorial. Philosophers had an answer, Sages and Saints had an answer, modern-day Psychologists have an answer, and all religions have an answer to this question. But unfortunately, the answer to this existential question is biased, or skewed to satisfy their own curiosity, or to sell their own paradigm about the individual human being. But each and every individual must ask this question to himself or herself as though his overall well-being, on this planet, depends upon the answer to this fundamental question because it truly depends on the answer to this question. That very question is:

WHO AM l?

Body, Mind and Awareness Complex

Awareness is like the sun. When it shines on things, they are transformed.

Thich Nhat Hanh (Nhat)

Understanding the spiritual relationship between body, mind and awareness is the key to total wellbeing of mankind. The ignorance of this crucial spiritual link between the trio, put us on the defensive, and we become enslaved to the circumstances. Knowledge of this spiritual relationship and its application in everyday life hold the key to open the doors of understanding and wisdom that every man or woman is in fact the architect of his or her destiny. All the enchanting forms of wealth like the great Taj Mahal or a piece of dazzling diamond can be reduced to energy dust, and one day all the formed matter will go back to its very source from where they all arose.

You are the Body

It is true that we all identify ourselves with our physical body, which we preserve with utmost care and concern, and our identity is encased in this vibrant physical entity. It is also true that this body is subject to pain, a sensation of suffering. Without pain, we cannot preserve this physical body. If we are made immune to pain, the body will become dysfunctional very soon, as we will ignore the sudden decay of the body for want of care and hygiene. Hence, the enlightened one declared "Pain is inevitable" (to the body) but suffering (a mental phenomenon) is optional. Reliving the pain again and again results in suffering, which can be avoided by careful introspection.

Who is responsible for our own body?

We are not a bag of chemicals or a bunch of bones, but an organism with intelligence which is immortal. Our physical body is a masterpiece in creation, and even the brightest scientist alive today cannot even replicate a very small piece of that body. Medical scientists all over the world are still discovering the mystery of every body part, and they are still baffled by the enormous simplicity with the body functions as a very efficient and able organism surviving our onslaught stemming from ignorance.

For a long time, medical researchers were not clear about the body mind relationship. But modern researchers are getting ahead of their predecessors in knowing in detail how both the body and the mind are working together to bring about physical and mental wellness to their base holders. It is the intelligence of the mind that is powering the body. Every thought that arises in the mind and dwelled upon constantly can change the biochemistry of the body.

With the help of functional MRI, brain researchers can witness the changes the brain goes through with differing mental transactions. Placebo effect has shown beyond scientific doubt that what a person believes to be true, has a lasting effect on the physical healing. Now the neuroscientist has enough evidence to prove that we can change the wiring of our brain using our mind. It will probably take another decade or so before the average person will start using the mind as a daily practice to bring about the healing to his physical body. Yes, it is the mind that powers our body.

You are your Mind!

Just like you identify with your body, you also identify with your mind. Mind is our instrument of perception. We need that instrument, which is a part and parcel of who we are, to perceive the objective world that is external to us. Once you understand the relationship with your mind, and its functions, you can effectively use the tool of transformation to reach wherever you want to reach. It is the total ignorance of the function of our mysterious instrument of perception, that causes suffering in our everyday life.

The eastern tradition and the many schools of thought proclaim that "you are not your mind". I beg to differ from the conventional wisdom and emphasize that you are the mind, because mind is an integral part of the body, mind awareness complex, that constitutes who you are, and who I am. Pure awareness or universal consciousness needs a medium to express itself and our body and mind provide the medium. Mind is the instrument of perception and body is the instrument of expression and when they operate in unison "I am born". So however efficient and powerful the awareness may be, it cannot express itself and be useful without my body and mind. Just like the brain is an integral part of my body and every thought is an integral part of my mind, awareness is also an integral part of 'being', which is generally described as my body, mind, and awareness complex. Understanding the relationship of body, mind, and awareness to each other is the key to have a purposeful and meaningful life on the planet. Just like the electric power cannot give us the light without it going through an electric bulb my awareness will have no impact on this planet except when it expresses itself through a body and mind apparatus. The body, mind, and awareness apparatus create my being which is named as Gopi Nair by my parents.

As I climb the rungs of the evolutionary ladder, I get a clearer and clearer picture of my whole being, the body, mind, and awareness complex. One day when awareness stops powering my mind, and the mind stops powering my body my children will say "Our dad is dead", which means my body, mind and awareness complex cannot function together as an organism, and the individual entity Gopi Nair, who once was alive and well, is no more. According to the custom, the body needs to be cremated, as it does not serve any purpose and starts to decay in the absence of the life force powering it. We can have the individual identity only if we have the body, mind, and awareness complex functioning as a total organism. It is essential for us to understand this organism, its structure, and functions before we can operate it efficiently.

You are also awareness

Your organism is only complete and ready to function when it is powered by a higher intelligence, which is also known as awareness. We are conscious of our body and mind because the mind is powered by awareness, the ultimate intelligence that power the universe, too. Awareness is undeniably the greatest power in the universe, but it cannot express itself without the medium of the mind and the body. We all can function effectively as human being only in the body powered by our mind, which in term is powered by awareness. In Hindu philosophy it is said "Isavasyam Idam Sarvom" (In Sanskrit), which means everything is the abode of God, the all-knowing awareness dwelling in slumber or live form in all that constitutes our universe. As we evolve through our body, mind, and awareness complex, we are understanding the operation of this being, commonly known as 'human being'. This understanding helps us to peel off the layers of ignorance one by one and realize our true self expressing itself through our mind and body.

Gratitude: A celebration of life

Gratitude is an attitude, probably the greatest attitude. It is embedded in pure optimism, always seeing the glass half full, not half empty. When you count your blessings and be grateful, you will attract more blessings to you. Thus, the half full glass can attract more of the same and make it full. It is sad that we do not understand the working of our own mind. The rich are getting richer, and the poor are becoming poorer, and most of us wonder why. It is the positive philosophy in action. Life is a self-fulfilling prophecy, as your thoughts, speech and action converge into your very experience. Since we do not know this fact, we blame everybody else for our shortcomings, lack of abundance, poverty, and poor health. While some of the programming in the childhood had some long-lasting effects even beyond childhood, we can overcome those programming, by rewiring our brain by changing our thoughts, speech, and action. The first and foremost important thing is to find our weakness and take action to cure those weaknesses.

Gratitude is the greatest Transformer

Gratitude is a time-tested change agent. It neutralizes negativity and take us to a positive path. It does not look for ways to complain, it does not blame anybody for our shortcomings. Gratitude begins with counting one's blessing one by one. No matter how bad our situation is, there are always some things to be grateful for. That is exactly where we begin, and that is exactly how we must begin to solve any problems.

Lord Jesus Christ had a big problem, after the Sermon on the Mount, because multitudes were following him, and they were weary, tired, and very hungry as they did not eat anything for a couple of days. Jesus knew that these hungry followers need to be fed and it was his moral responsibility. So, he asked the apostles, "what have we got in the house"? "Five loaves of bread and two fishes" replied the apostles. Bring them to me, Jesus commanded them. He took the five loaves and two fishes and lifted them towards the heavens and thanked. He then commanded the apostles to make the people sit on the grass and start serving them. There were five thousand followers who were fed, and still there were twelve baskets of food left. So, whatever may be your problem, accept it and give thanks to your higher power and abundance will appear. Gratitude removes the negativity of lack and doubt, which pave the way for the new blessings to come in. No matter what your problem is, start giving thanks for whatever blessings you enjoy, and more blessings will follow. Most of us look for (habitually) what we are missing in life and focus on that. Because we are giving our awareness to the lack, the more of the same will fill our life. But if you consciously look, you will find a list of things for which you can be grateful. That must be the starting point. When we are focusing on the blessings we have, like the good wife or husband, loving parents, or robust health we enjoy or the good job, we are shifting our focus. Gratitude is a celebration of life, because we are remembering the good things for which we are grateful. This is the best psychotherapy for abundance of health, wealth, and happiness. Praise the lord of your understanding (praise positively raise), and give thanks for the things you have, more will be added to you. Gratitude is the mother of all positive emotions like respect, appreciation, empathy, kindness, and forgiveness.

Gratitude, the starting point

We all can use gratitude as a starting point to embark on a voyage of transformation. We do not have to wait for something to happen to alleviate our suffering and claim our birth right to peace and plenty. When we start our quest for a change, with expressing the gratitude for all that we have, even insignificant things, we are opening the floodgates of abundance in health, wealth, and peace of mind.

The Art of Giving

The secret of receiving is the art of giving. Whatever you want to receive in your life, you start giving that to anybody who crosses your path. Hence, all religion prescribes giving charity because there is a science behind that. When you give something, you are happy about it, and giving is also the symbol of abundance. Giving is a pleasing act that will reverberate through your entire being. Almost all the religions prescribe some kind of tithing, usually a small percentage of one's income, as a mark of our own gratitude towards the Creator. If we are all the children of the same god, we are helping our brothers and sisters who need of our help. It is another way to honor the glory of God and appreciate the good blessings we enjoy in our life. But when we give something to a needy person, it is imperative that we do not judge that person and feel proud that we are giving money or other help to another. If your ego swells because of the charity that you offer, it defeats the very purpose. Always remember the hand that gives, is the hand of God, and we need to feel humble whenever we offer anything to help a needy person.

Humility is the very essence of tithing.

Do you know the secret of receiving?

The secret of receiving lies in the art of giving! Do not forget this as long as you are living. Universe is a principle; it runs on The Law of Reciprocity! To call it plainly raw, whatever you want in life write it down, it could be name, fame or even the crown. Start taking actions, take baby steps of giving, giving from your heart, is the soul of receiving. Do you want to make a million Dollars? The same law applies, give away dollars distribute one dollar to everyone, practice giving Universe will surely reciprocate. You learn to live your life by this simple rule everything multiples after its kind, very cool. Are you looking for more love in your life? Start giving your love to everyone without strife. Do not be a beggar begging for things to come. You command the universe, sure is the outcome, but you must obey the law, The Law of Reciprocity! It works in London, Lucknow and in every city. Now that you know the secret of receiving, start practicing it. Knowledge is utterly useless if it is not practiced in everyday life. Make your knowledge a habit, and it will earn you dividends in kind throughout your life. Can you make your everyday life filled with the art of giving? You might ask, "I am poor, I have nothing to give, not even a dollar". We all can give everyone a big smile, to uplift and inspire another soul going through worse problem, than you can imagine. We can use kind words, and expressions to encourage every soul crossing your path. You can give your time, which otherwise you may be spending to brood over your problems, to a soup kitchen to serve the food to the hungry and less fortunate lining up in front of the soup kitchen every weekend. You can read a story to your sister's son, or your own daughter if you have one. If you do not have too much money, that is ok. But when you go to your temple, church synagogue or mosque over the weekend try to put some change in the donation box. More than the money, the feelings behind the giving are going to rewire your brain and make transformation very possible and real. You can rewire your brain to a prosperous and wealthy brain, by using the power of neuroplasticity. Change your thoughts, change your words, and change your deeds reflecting the art of giving, you are rewiring your brain to receive more blessings in life.

"Ask you shall receive, seek you shall find, knock it shall be opened unto you", are not hollow words, as they are pregnant with profound meaning and philosophical truth. Every prayer, no matter to which religion it belongs to, is nothing but an expression of gratitude. Lord Jesus Christ, like many other spiritual teachers, from every tradition, used to pray regularly. Prayer is a psychotherapy to prepare your mind to reduce the negativity and infuse with hope and optimism. The best treatment for every human mind is a dose of inspiration in the morning especially before you kick off the day.

Long time ago there lived a peasant in a small village in India. He was very religious and believed in the power of prayer. During the monsoon season, one day the floodwaters were rushing through the village, threatening his small house that stood on the banks of a small river. Water started accumulating, and water level rushed up to the knee level. The village volunteers came to help him out of his house with his belongings. He refused the help, saying that he prayed God, and "god will save me". He continued praying, and the water level continued to rise to his shoulder, and another rescue team came with a boat and asked him to get in. He would not step into the boat with the same argument that "I am praying god, and god will save me". As the water continued to rise, the farmer climbed on the roof of the house to escape the rushing water. Then a helicopter appeared above the house, and the rescue team asked him to pull the rope they threw from the helicopter. The stubborn peasant refused to do so and said, "I am praying god, and he will take care of me". Finally, the rushing floodwaters consumed him, and he found himself standing in front of St Peter.

Bewildered and shocked, the farmer asked St Peter, "Why didn't god save me"? Didn't he hear my prayers, he asked repeatedly St Peter looked at the peasant with sympathy and in a tender voice said "when you pray to God, God will answer your prayer for sure. God works through his children who are chosen for the purpose. Your neighbor, the fireman and the helicopter pilot were all commissioned by God alone to rescue you. But you did not trust them, or even God for that matter.

So next time, when you pray, believe that God will answer your prayer He will commission his trusted children for the mission. Please listen to the signals from the universe! You, too, are a chosen child of God to help others who are confronted by similar dangers. Many times, you have an urge to talk to someone or help someone. This is how God gets his work done, through you and me.

Be patient with God!

While you are looking for the signals from the universe, you and I need to be patient to receive the answers to our prayers. You are not His only problem, I am not His only problem, to say the least about the workload of the God. After you have "asked" spiritually by means of your prayer, not only be patient, get busy with your day-to-day routine, without dwelling on the problem. If at all any doubts creep into your consciousness, as they are likely to, just recite three times "I am grateful for the experience". A dose of gratitude at the nick of time is absolutely necessary to cleanse your mind and cast off the doubts. These are time tested principles of psychotherapy, and they do work if you allow it to work, in terms of your own patience and your own unshaken faith in the power of prayer. It happens every day, in every part of the world, and to people belonging to every religion or faith, to people regardless of the color of the skin.

The prayer of an old Indian mother

One day in the south Indian state of Kerala where I come from, an elephant got out of control and started running ransacking things around. Every year this happens in Kerala, when elephants are brought in as a part of the temple festival. Now there are laws to prevent cruelty to elephants, and the way they are transported to long distances. This must have happened, may be thirty years ago. This mad elephant was destroying everything on its path and ransacked a small hut , and the old mother who was living alone was wakened up from her deep sleep by the commotion. When she opened her eyes, she saw an elephant standing in front of her, and she first thought she was only dreaming. She cleared her eyes and looked, and she realized that she was in real danger. She did not know what to do, and in her despair, she cried out "my son, please do not kill me". The cry of prayer from a shaken mother.

The story, as told by the old mother, has a happy ending. The mad elephant stopped ransacking the house and simply walked away from the old mother and her hut. While I was not there when it happened, as I live in Chicago, but I happened to know this old mother and her family as they lived in my own neighborhood. An amazing story, you can interpret it in any way you want, but the fact is that even the wild elephant listens to a heartfelt prayer, that too from a mother.

Practice Self-Awareness

Practice of self-awareness is the key to emotional freedom. We have political freedom, and economic freedom, besides religious freedom, and the freedom of speech. But we cannot enjoy any of this freedom unless we have emotional freedom. All other freedom is built on the freedom from emotional slavery. Self-awareness is the art of reminding us of who we are, we are this body, we are this mind, and we are the awareness, the consciousness. Constantly dwell on the truth that our body is powered by our mind, and our mind is powered by the pure awareness. Pure awareness or the consciousness, which is self-effulgent, as it is the ultimate light powering the universe. It is infinite, it is not born, and therefore it does not die. It is immortal, eternal beyond name, quality, and color, The ancient Rishis of India who were the master of mind, and self-awareness, called it "atman" or soul and that which is indivisible. The whole universe is pervaded by this pure energy, that is powering our mind, the mind in turn powers our very body, which is visible to us, in which we all dwell.

"This body is the temple of the living god" declared Lord Jesus Christ, who was also a master of self-awareness. As we climb the ladder of our own evolution we recognize, our body the physical form, our mind the creator of thoughts and emotions and our very instrument of perception. Having experienced the secret of our bodily and mental faculties, we are ready to experience the ultimate consciousness, or the pure awareness by knowing which there is nothing more to know in this universe. Until we reach the state of pure consciousness, we identify with our body, our mind, and few glimpses of awareness. But pure awareness can exist without the body or the mind, but it is useless to function in this world without the physical body and its powering mind. The four-year-old little girl puts two pebbles as the teacher instructed, with another two pebbles to get the knowledge two plus two equals to four. By the time she reaches second or third grade, she does not need those four pebbles to calculate two plus two equals to four. The same little girl will learn algebra, calculus, and advanced algebra when she is in the senior year of high school. When she goes on to the college and climb the ladder of mathematical knowledge, she uncovers the very secret of the mathematical creation and is capable of discovering the new mathematical formulas of her own. But today she is the four-year-old girl who needs these four pebbles to calculate two plus two is equal to four.

The same way today, we are like the four-year-old girl learning the primary lessons of our own existence as the body and mind. Thus, we realize that we are this body, we are this mind, both being powered by the all-knowing awareness. The existence of their ultimate power of awareness is only known at the intellectual level, and not at the emotional level, where we can experience the oneness with all other creatures. That is the point when the veil of separation collapses, and we come to the rude realization that it is the same power that is dwelling in me is the same power dwelling in you, and even moving a small blade of grass. This is the 'eureka' moment when Jesus Christ realized that "me and my father are one".

When you know who you are, when I know who I am, evolution is complete. 'Myness' and 'Yourness' will collapse, and 'mine' and "yours' mentality will only exist in the pages of the mortal past. After having realized this very essence of our existence, we only live for the purpose of uplifting the world, by our service and the very presence. The darkness of ignorance will start fading away by the very presence of the light of knowledge. The body will have to perish and wither away into five elements, as everybody will go back to the source from where it came. Being immortal does not mean your body is immortal. It only means your identification splits from your body to the all-knowing awareness, the pure consciousness, which was never born, therefore it will never die. This is the state of immortality where our false identification with the body collapses, and you become fearless of death itself, as it can annihilate your physical existence. If you do not identify with your body, death cannot threaten you. Still the attachment to the body is life long, and even at the last moments approach when the life force or prana is withdrawn from the body, the pain of separation from the body is unbearable. Even Lord Jesus Christ, according to recorded history, cried out aloud "father have you forsaken me"?

The truth is that one day the body has to give in and say, enough is enough' and the mortal frame is made up of five elements to which the body eventually returns. But today as you look at yourself you are the body, that is powered by your mind, which is the instrument of perception. Mind is the playground of awareness that all knowing awareness, the deathless entity, which was never born, so that it will not die. As we climb the ladder of evolution, it is possible for us to attain one hundred percent realization (self) the awareness turning on itself. It is called the "witness within". Even when you are thinking about a thing, you are aware that you are thinking. In fact, you are looking at the thinker within, as a witness. Separating you from the thought is a time-tested technique of self-realization, the sense of the ultimate truth of your nature. Once the relationship between body, mind and awareness is clear within yourself, it is the collapse of unconscious living, and once we all come to know who we are, evolution is complete. It is the ultimate knowledge, by knowing which everything else in the universe becomes an open book for you and me.

There was, once, lived a Hindu devotee of Vishnu, one of the three deities, also known as 'three Murthy', who wanted to reach and take refuge in him as the ultimate salvation. He prayed and prayed all his life, he observed all the religious austerities, observed silence as and when required according to the Hindu scriptures. He undertook pilgrimages to holy places, chanting the hymns of Vishnu ceaselessly. As he removed his layers of ignorance also called Maya in Sanskrit, which means veil, veil that covers the reality, by his penances and clear thinking. He performed selfless service for the benefit of mankind, with absolutely no selfish motive, except to get freedom from the thralldom of flesh. At the end of his spiritual journey, searching the entire lifetime, he came to the stunning realization that the Lord Vishnu whom he was searching for day and night, was indeed he himself. The veil of ignorance or the layers of ignorance were removed one by one the devotee could become Vishnu, the all-knowing God of his choice, came clearer and clearer to him. The same view of oneness with God was echoed by Lord Jesus Christ when he declared, 'me and my father are one'.

"Look Within"

There was a beggar sitting on a dilapidated wooden box in a small village in India, and a saint was passing that way. The beggar asked the holy man "Sir give me something, I'm poor" the holy man said, "I am like you, I have nothing to give". He asked the beggar, "what are you sitting on". It is just a useless box; I have been sitting on it ever since I can remember. Another holy man gave it to me years ago when I started begging! Came the reply. "Did you ever care to look in", asked again, the holy man. "Let us open it and see" urged the saint and upon his prompting, the beggar began to open the wooden box. There were layers of old newspapers, then came old clothes, and some pieces of stones. After removing all these seemingly ancient and useless 'stuff, the beggar saw a very old pouch. The holy man asked the beggar to open the pouch. The beggar followed the instruction and took out the contents of the pouch. The beggar could not believe his eyes. There were five, fine, dazzling gold coins in the old pouch hidden beneath the bottom of the dilapidated wooden box.

The moral of the story is that almost all of us seldom know what we are sitting on. We are all looking for answers elsewhere, for our problems just like that beggar. In fact we used to, and we ought to "look within". All the wealth of the world, all the gold you and I need are all hidden in the form of ideas that are hidden in the sacred vault of our subconscious mind, the seat of our memory. The subconscious is the powerful ally of the conscious mind, which is the master mind. We all have the ability to imagine what we want and hold on to the imagination and pour our 'awareness' at regular intervals to convert the energy into matter. Matter is nothing but energy in its condensed form, and energy is nothing but matter in its purest form. We can redirect our own thoughts into any directions we want, to create any form of wealth we desire. We have been doing it already in our life, and without the knowledge of the universal Law of Reciprocity. Furthermore, we have been creating only, despair, despondency at the emotional level, and piling up bills and debts at the financial level. Once you understand The Law of Reciprocity and look within you too can discover the gold pieces like that penniless beggar who was sitting on gold, which he thought was a dilapidated wooden box.

Points to Ponder:

1. The ultimate thinking ends up with an essential question.

2. Who am I? We all need to ask this question

3. Am I this body?

4. Am I this mind?

5. Am I the awareness who powers the mind?

6. We are indeed a complete organism.

7. Body, Mind Awareness Complex

8. An understanding of the relationship between these three components can shed more light to the existential question, who am I?

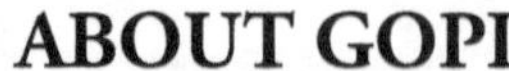

ABOUT GOPI

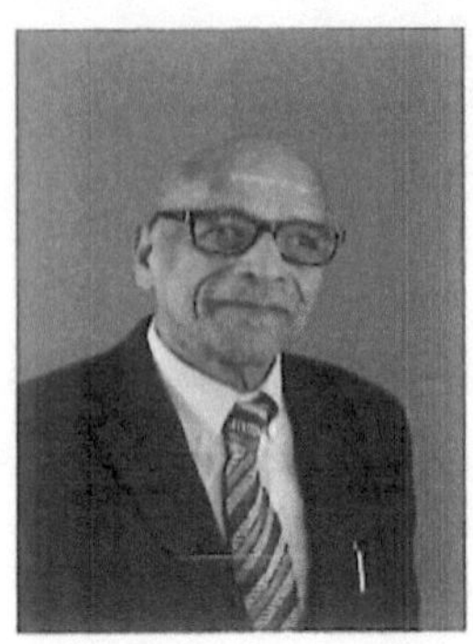

Gopi has been a Gratitude Practitioner, embarked on a mission to change lives for the better, by encouraging every one to practice Gratitude. Gopi is convinced that Gratitude is a magic wand capable of removing negativity from the shores of human mind! Devoid of negativity and its energy draining consequences, any one can realize his or her full potential. "Gratitude must be the only attitude in life" is Gopi's mantra. He thinks Gratitude, speaks Gratitude and relentlessly does Deeds of Gratitude in every day life. We all can give the gift of Gratitude to others to enrich their lives along with ours!

Gopi has been in sales for over four decades, and that gave him an opportunity to interact with thousands of people. He used his insight into emotional wisdom to navigate through the world of sales, successfully. While he was working with Metlife, he qualified three times for the prestigious Presidents Conference, and several times for the Million Dollar Round Table. During his career with Metlife, he trained several Agents in his capacity as a Manager.

During the last twenty years Gopi has been a Mortgage Broker with Homeland Mortgage Company. He worked with Guaranteed Rate as a Vice President of Mortgage Lending for two years.

Gopi is a Best Selling Author, and published ten books like Mental Science 101, Manage your Mind, Manage Your Life, How I made 50000 in Selling at Age 69, and Tablets of Emotional Wisdom. Gopi's Gratitude Journal was published in 2021, and a Gratitude Journal for Every Father in 2023.Gopi's Philosophy of Life can be summarized in one sentence "when you live for yourself, life is utterly miserable, when you live for others, it is pure joy". Gopi had the privilege of being interviewed by Jack Canfield, the famous author and creator of the Chicken Soup for the Soul, about his book Tablets of Emotional Wisdom.

Gopi graduated from the University of Bombay with a Master's degree in business. He migrated to the States almost half a century ago. He is an Inspirational Speaker, always willing and available to speak about the Power of Gratitude in changing lives. You can contact Gopi at 630-290-6847, or gopi132@yahoo.com.

www.ingramcontent.com/pod-product-compliance
Lightning Source LLC
Chambersburg PA
CBHW032232050726
47591CB00001B/364

9781962484350